АЛЬМАНАХ
ЖЕНЩИНАМ О ЖЕНЩИНАХ
ВЫПУСК 1

10 ДЕКАБРЯ 1979 г

ALMANACH

for women about women
number one

10 December 1979

Sheba Feminist Publishers

Woman and Russia was first published in the USSR in December, 1979 and was published in a translation from the russian in September, 1980 by Sheba Feminist Publishers, London.

© The Almanach authors, © the translation, the Women and Eastern Europe Group.

Typeset by Frances and Lin of Range Left Photosetters, tel. 01-739 0296.

Printed by A. Wheaton & Co. Ltd., Exeter.

Cover design by An Dekker.

ISBN 0 907179 02 9

Women and Eastern Europe Group

We are a group of women who believe that to study the position of women in Eastern Europe is important to us both as feminists and as socialists. The women's movement has not traditionally paid much attention to the Soviet Union, partly because there is no organised women's movement there. Yet the Soviet Union calls itself socialist and asserts that it has solved the 'woman question'. It is up to us to demonstrate that this is untrue, that the subordinate position of women is as integral to the political system in the East as it is in the West, and to use the discussion of the position of women in the Soviet Union to inform debates within the women's movement here.

We can be contacted through Sheba.

Introduction

In January of this year we heard that a feminist samizdat ("self-printed and published") journal was circulating in Leningrad and had been smuggled out to France. We were at once very excited, very curious, and surprised. For although dissident publications surface in the Soviet Union fairly frequently, they are written mostly by men and have shown little interest in the specific position of women. Moreover, the many women active in the dissident movement have up until now considered the particular problems of women – if they exist – to be marginal to the struggle in which they are engaged. We had always felt sure that these attitudes would change. But knowing the prejudices against feminism within Soviet society as a whole, we thought change might take some time coming.

In the Soviet Union all political and social organisations have to be initiated and directed by the party or the state. Women's magazines are published, but there is no women's movement. From our own limited contact with Soviet society we have had to guess at the changing attitudes of Soviet women, their hopes and aspirations. Soviet sociologists do undertake surveys on women's leisure activities, their domestic labour; demographers assemble daunting tables of birth rates and family size; and journalists write about morals, marriage and the family. But the questions they ask and the answers they find are cramped and inhibited by censorship and the political system. The rising number of women seeking divorce does suggest that women are no longer willing to accept family problems as a fact of life, and questions about personal relationships have been raised by the press more frequently these last few years. Still, even reading between the lines it is not easy to be sure which way things are moving. That is why we were so pleased to hear that a feminist journal had appeared. For our group, which has been discussing the situation of Soviet women for a number of years now, this was the first tangible evidence of change and of some women to whom we could respond, and with whom we could perhaps exchange ideas and experience.

1

Exactly what kind of changes the Almanach would represent we had no idea. We knew nothing about the editors of *Woman and Russia*, whether or not they might, like one Polish dissident group, be in favour of banning abortion. We wondered anxiously whether we would feel at home with their feminism. Finally, a photo-copy of the Almanach appeared from Paris – 130-odd pages of articles, short stories and poetry, the print faint in places and difficult to decipher. Some of the contents we found difficult to appreciate; we felt distant from the religious ideas expressed by one or two of the women and we shuddered at the conservative ideas in Tat'yana Goricheva's article. But on the whole, to our relief, the Almanach spoke a language we could understand.

The editors of the Almanach have apparently had little contact with the Western women's movement. Though they refer to sexism, talk about the onset of phallocracy, and mention Gay Liberation, they suggest, in their introduction, that in the West the woman question is well on the way to being solved. Their feminism cannot have come from the West. Neither has it come to them from the past. Apart from a couple of favourable passing references to the Russian revolution and to Lenin, they seem not to be aware of historical roots. They write about themselves and draw examples and conclusions from their own personal experience. The Almanach stands in a sense apart from society and from history; it starts from the individual woman's sense of bitterness and betrayal that her life should be the way it is. In this, *Woman and Russia* is very close to some of the early writings of the Western women's movement and to the tradition of personal testimony which is still strong.

Although the Almanach does not express itself as part of a longer tradition of feminist thinking and organising, it is still illuminating to look at the history of feminism in Russia and to situate the Almanach within some sort of broader historical context. Certainly the Almanach is not the first expression of Russian feminism. For Soviet women – as for women in the West – our history has been hidden. In the Soviet Union there are perhaps particular reasons for this, since feminism has always been identified as bourgeois in its class interests, and has been met by the Communist Party with suspicion and hostility.

The history of feminism in Russia stretches back to the early nineteenth century, but it emerged as a political philosophy and movement during the 1905 revolution, basing itself on liberal virtues such as self-reliance and self-education, and demanding liberal reforms: the vote and access to the professions for propertied women, freer divorce and legitimacy laws, an end to alcoholism and militarism, the death penalty and state-licensed prostitution, and improvements in the conditions under which women worked. The Bolsheviks believed that to propose such a programme of reforms without acknowledging the need for social revolution – to attempt to 'liberalise' tsarism – was dangerous nonsense. A very small number of marxist women at this time urged women workers to find their allies in women within the revolutionary socialist movement rather than with these feminists – who were sometimes their employers and had different class interests. But when these marxist women went on to urge the revolutionary movement to recognise the double oppression of working women, many men in the movement were quick to attack them as 'feminists' trying to introduce 'sexual divisions' into the united working class and its party. Very few Bolsheviks seriously attempted to go further than giving the women vague assurances that socialist revolution would automatically remove all forms of oppression, including the oppression of women. In the years before the revolution, the needs of women were not *integrated* into the Bolshevik political programme.

After October 1917, after women strikers and street-fighters had written themselves too prominently into revolutionary history to be ignored any longer, various leading Bolshevik women succeeded in organising a women's congress in Petrograd, from which a party-backed women's commission emerged. This was so popular that in 1920 the commission was upgraded to the status of a women's department of the party (*zhenotdel*), and soon virtually every European province in the Soviet union had its own women's department.

Women began to discuss the best ways of organising communal state-supported nurseries for their children, as well as tackling such questions as abortion, prostitution and venereal disease. However, as the women's department, under its radical new director Alexandra Kollontai, set about solving these and many other issues in a series of inspiring campaigns aimed to transform women's everyday lives, it gained many enemies. All too often women were prevented from taking up their delegates' posts in the unions until the party had intervened on their behalf. And although it became a 'counter-revolutionary offence' for men to beat up women – and women who attended political meetings were often singled out in particular – the practice still continued.

After the introduction of the New Economic Policy in 1921[1], unemployment became widespread and women were the first to lose their jobs. Money to fund creches, canteens and the women's department was withdrawn. In 1922 the women's department's staff was reduced from forty to twenty-one, and Alexandra Kollontai was replaced by a less radical director. It was in response to this that various unofficial women's papers began to circulate at that time: dreaded 'bourgeois feminism' once more reared its ugly head, was jumped on heavily by the official press, and eventually stifled by the party.

So despite its many imaginative campaigns – to change the laws on marriage, prostitution and abortion, to set up women's literacy programmes, and encourage Moslem women to abandon their veils – the women's department had always been answerable to the party whose interests it served. The party had always been mistrustful of women organizing together. To a certain extent this was due to its confusing feminism with 'bourgeois feminism', but it was also because Bolshevik men were reluctant to confront their own sexism and to accept the personal and political implications of an autonomous women's movement. During the early '20s, women won for themselves a political voice, but as the popular enthusiasm generated by the revolution evaporated, and as the party gained absolute control over political life, and itself became more authoritarian, the women's movement faltered.

The party began to urge that the women's department co-ordinate its activities more closely with those of the agitprop department – which effectively meant its increased subordination to the party. In 1930 it announced that separate women's organisations were no longer necessary, that women were sufficiently liberated to fend for themselves. The close of the *zhenotdel* was part of a general shift in Soviet political life. The trade unions, the youth organisations, the local party branches, lost their independence and political power. The central committee ruled alone, demanding absolute obedience and conformity.

The Bolshevik leadership proclaimed that socialism could be built in one country, and set out to achieve this goal by forcing collectivisation of agriculture and industrialisation from above. The needs of individual social groups were subordinated to the economic targets of the Five Year Plans. The Women's Day slogan for 1929 was "For 100% Collectivisation". Ideas about alternative lifestyles and socialising housework, discussed during the 1920s, were now branded as dangerously utopian and petit bourgeois. Huge women's meetings were held to proclaim the importance of the family and to assure women that their equality was already a reality. Women's main right and duty was now to provide the future workforce for the social transformation of the Soviet Union. The leading article in *Pravda* May 28, 1936 expressed the new ideology of heroic motherhood: "A woman without children merits our pity for she does not know the full joy of life. Our Soviet women, full-blooded citizens of the freest country in the world, have been given the bliss of motherhood. We must safeguard our family and raise and rear healthy Soviet heroes." That same year, abortion – legal since 1920 – was outlawed.

The cult of motherhood was promoted by the regime throughout the Stalin period. It was only in 1955, during the period of relaxation following the death of Stalin in 1953, known as the Thaw, that the Soviet Union adopted the policy of 'conscious motherhood': abortion once again became legal, and the government promised to increase childcare facilities. However, it is the area of maternity provision which has provoked the bitterest criticism from the women writing in the Almanach.

They are angry not about the lack of abortion clinics and nurseries – things we in this country are still fighting for – but about the quality of care in these state-run institutions. When it comes to spending money, they are given a low priority compared to defence and industry. As in the whole of the service sector, the staff – usually women – are both overworked and underpaid, and come under a lot of pressure. As a result, hostile and unsympathetic attitudes are widespread – not just in clinics, but in shops, on buses, and in queues everywhere. But it is during the vulnerable time of pregnancy, when control over our bodies passes into the hands of others, that women are likely to feel this unkindness most acutely.

Estimates say that on average Soviet women have five or six

pregnancies. Yet most women give birth to only one child, or at the most two. Contraception is available, but it is not well-publicised and often methods are crude (uncomfortable IUDs, high-dosage pills, unreliable condoms and spermicides). The habit of relying on abortion, which took a strong hold in the '20s when it was legal and there was little alternative, has never really been challenged. Some Western writers have put the number of abortions performed each year as high as eight million. Quite a few are done illegally by women who fear the kind of conditions described in the Almanach, who want to keep the abortion secret, or who are outside the permitted time limits. An unofficial abortion is performed by doctors in hospital or in a private flat, for the payment of a modest fee, and more modern methods such as vacuum-suction are often used. It is another aspect of the ever-present corruption, known as *blat*, which runs throughout Soviet life.

It can also be found in nurseries – *The Other Side of the Medal* mentions the way in which the best food is pilfered – and in the maternity homes, where money or connections can be used to gain more sympathetic treatment. This can make a real difference during childbirth, as husbands and friends are totally excluded from the event. All births are hospitalised; rural women may even be moved many miles in labour. No visitors are allowed into the maternity homes, so the new father will not even see the baby until it is a week old. The women are isolated from networks of support, and their sole responsibility for the baby is taken for granted. Going through labour in isolation is hard for anyone; for an unprepared woman it must indeed be a nightmare.

Ironically, it was the Soviet Union which first developed the 'psycho-prophylactic' method of preparation for childbirth which has since become the basis of natural childbirth in the West. In the early years of the revolution doctors challenged the belief that women ought to suffer in labour, and began to search for effective methods of pain relief. Psychoprophylaxis was adopted as national policy in 1951, and official reports say that now about two-thirds of women use it. (They also say that over 90% use this or another method of pain-relief; the trend is towards more technological childbirth.) In practice this may only mean that a woman has attended a couple of ante-natal classes (time off work is not given). Unless she is well-prepared, supported throughout, and finds that her personal autonomy is respected, psychoprophylaxis is unlikely to work well. Psychoprophylaxis in the West assumes the involvement and support of a close companion. But in the Soviet Union, a mother is allowed no one with her. At worst she is simply left and told to get on with it – as in *Human Birth*. This account shows that, though injections of some kind may be given, the level of technical help and even basic comfort can be very low.

A woman's problems are not over when the baby arrives. Financially, it can be a difficult time. Paid maternity leave is only for fifty-six days after the birth (and fifty-six before). The various benefits for unmarried mothers and low-income families are far from generous, (eg twelve roubles per month for children under eight years in families with a per capita income of less than fifty roubles).[2] Women can go back to work when the paid leave ends, and if they wish to continue breastfeeding they are allowed half an hour every four hours for doing so. But many spend the whole first year at home. There is concern about the quality of care in creches for young babies, and the fact that the infant mortality rate, unpublished since 1974, appears to be rising, seems to confirm this. Mothers out of step with the official ideology have even more reason to distrust state care.

In 1977 the government decided to make spending on maternity care and children's hospitals a priority within the health service. Change may come, especially as the government is increasingly worried about the low birth-rate – one result of women's easy access to abortion. But in practice these measures are limited, and instead the government relies on cajolement and flattery. Women are 'mother heroines' still, and the nation is grateful for their 'great and noble work'. The problems of combining motherhood with full-time work are lightly dismissed: "It is in woman's character readily to take on a large and varied load".

It is worth looking at the formative role the press plays in moulding this 'New Soviet Woman'. One of its devices, particularly in mass circulation women's magazines, is to present the ideal woman who is at one and the same time ordinary and exemplary: ordinary in that she is the type of woman in the type of occupation that the reader might encounter daily; exemplary in that she displays the desired attributes of the 'New Soviet Woman'. She is responsible about her job, cares for her family, and is also active in the community. Women's magazines discuss the problems arising from such a combination only in terms of strengthening the family at an individual level: women must encourage their husbands to participate more in domestic life. But men themselves never read these articles. And only publications directed at women carry articles on cooking, domestic management and childcare.

The propaganda starts young: a survey of children's readers done in 1971-2 shows women as "nurturing, expressive of emotion, watching, listening, supportive of others". Women are seen as mothers first: women have jobs and men have careers. From the time they are at school, little girls are encouraged to fulfill a mother-role. They are regarded as a stabilising influence because they internalize society's values and use them to exert a good influence on the more unruly, but creative and independent boys. As many girls as boys go on to higher education, but most study humanities, leaving science to male students. The professions in which women predominate, such as teaching and medicine, are not held in very high esteem. Among Soviet women there is the expectation that they will work and the reasons given are not very different from those one hears in the West – extra cash, companionship, status. But there is fierce competition for the limited number of good jobs and much frustration from working in undesired and boring ones.

Men and women's political involvement tends to parallel sex role differences learned in the family. Women tend to do routine, secretarial tasks, while men make the decisions. Women are active in local party branches, but absent at provincial and national levels. The editorial collective of the Almanach claims that men fear women's competition, especially in areas of leadership. There is also the problem of women's low self-esteem. Essentially, women must always put their families first. If they dare to step outside their allotted roles they know they will have to pay for it.

In 1969 a story appeared in the journal *Novy Mir* which caused a great stir.[3] The author, Natalya Baranskaya, describes 'A Week Like Any Other' in the life of one young working mother, a week that typifies the experience of thousands of other young working mothers across the Soviet Union. The main character is harassed by worries about shopping, cooking, taking the children to and from the creche, and holding down a job in a laboratory. Her husband scarcely contributes to the family's struggle for survival.

A Soviet woman's daily reality is certainly harsh. Shopping especially is a burden. Although self-service shops are on the increase, they still involve queuing – even queuing to pay at the cashdesk, and then queuing again at separate counters in the same store for different items. Distribution of goods is poor, and people will queue hours if they see something that is in short supply: toilet paper or the first oranges of the winter. You rarely see men in queues. Living conditions don't make life easier. Many families have no hot water or electricity, let alone washing machines or refrigerators. The communal flats mentioned in the Almanach are not experiments in collective living: families are forced to live in the same flat, sharing the kitchen and toilet, for lack of adequate housing.

Given all this, personal relationships would be hard enough. The situation is worsened by the extent of alcoholism among men. (The husband's alcoholism is given as the reason for divorce in up to 40% of all divorces.) Drinking is at the heart of male culture. It excludes and degrades women, as does the constant use of obscene swear words which revolve round 'mother fucking'. It is difficult to convey to a non-Russian speaker the hatred of women encased in these expressions. Motherhood is extolled by the politicians and desecrated by the abusive language of everyday life. The paradox is well summed up in the Russian proverb: "A woman is an evil no house should be without".

The reaction of the 'woman in the kitchen' to this state of affairs has been given voice recently in various newspapers. Not fooled by the clamour surrounding March 8 – International Women's Day – their one big day a year, Soviet women responded bitterly to a husband's complaint, published in the weekly *Literaturnaya Gazeta*, that his wife didn't look after him properly and refused to do all the housework. The *Gazeta* took the husband's side, asking 'Where Do Bad Wives Come From?'. Enraged letters flooded in from women, with tales of alcoholic and indifferent husands and fathers. According to one woman, "The image of the Soviet father, building a model with his son, or going out with the children is a myth. More often than not he slumps in front of the telly and watches sport."

Clearly, some Soviet women are becoming more critical. But they have no organisations, no movement through which to voice their anger and make demands. Of course, there is no real opening for *any* oppressed group within the Soviet Union – ethnic minorities for example – to express criticisms or fight for change. Indeed, there are no working class organisations which are not completely incorporated into the state. The trade unions are basically concerned with welfare and social work. They do not have any real control over planning production or over the labour process, and do not provide any forum for political debate or pressure for change. In fact, the only organised opposition within the Soviet Union is the unofficial and heavily repressed dissident movement, of which the Almanach authors are inevitably a part. (It is significant that they call their Almanach *Woman and Russia*, not *the Soviet Union*, and say it comes from St Petersburg, not Leningrad, on December 10, 1979 – the anniversary of the International Declaration of the Rights of Man.)

The dissident movement known to its supporters as the 'democratic movement', is a heterogeneous collection of people who have been forced into opposition to the Soviet regime for many different reasons. All of them demand civil rights; freedom of expression, of association, of religion, of the press. They also demand that the Soviet Union observe its own constitution and the international agreements it has signed – such as the Helsinki Final Act. Further than this, however, dissidents differ in how they see the future of the Soviet system. Some, like Alexander Solzhenitsyn, look to Russia's past, denouncing godless Soviet communism. Others, like Andrei Sakharov, while opposing the system in its present form, think it can be democratised from within. Still others, like the student 'Left Opposition' which recently surfaced in Leningrad, want a revolution to sweep it all away. And there are also many dissidents who start from specific grievances – nationalists; members of persecuted religious groups; workers who want the right to be able to form free trade unions; artists and writers who don't want to conform to the deadening cultural uniformity which the system prescribes.

The writers of the Almanach are not working class and with one exception they come from Russia, the main republic in the Soviet Union. They are members of the intelligentsia exposed to the same intellectual currents that thave shaped the ideas of the dissident movement as a whole. Some of the women have been influenced by religious ideas and nearly all are artists of some kind. In Soviet society both religion and art can be seen as a counterweight to official values. Many people, educated to be atheists, have turned to religion as a way of finding individual spiritual satisfaction and fulfillment. Tat'yana Goricheva describes in the Almanach how, disillusioned with the emptiness of her life, she was converted to christianity. For several years now she has been active in the religious underground, organising seminars and writing on philosophical and psychological themes. She is one of the editors of a religous samizdat journal *37*, to which Evgeniya Shvarts, the translator of the *Mahadevi*, has contributed her own poetry.

Because Russia has never had a 'rational' revolution, an enlighten-ment or a renaissance, religion[4] has always played a far more important part in liberal intellectual life there than it has in the West. In their journeys 'to the people' in the 1860s, women revolutionaries were often treated with a great deal more respect by the non-conformist religous communities they visited than they were by their own male comrades. But it was in the chaotic spirit of enquiry following the 1905 revolution that revolution and religion became interchangeably fused in the minds of many 'seeking marxists' and 'Godseekers'. Some Bolsheviks began seriously to discuss the validity of religious experience and to stress the communism inherent in christianity. Many who had demonstrated with red flags as mystical anarchists in 1905 would later join religious groups which renounced politeness, the police, and concerts, sexual relation-ships, medicine. Yet despite all the irrationality and idealism of these religous groups, they shared with the Bolsheviks a revulsion against hypocrisy and philistinism; religious anarchists and atheist revolutionaries discovered they had much in common. Moreover, Russia's religious traditions, interrupted by the Bolshevik revolution, were revived both by those intellectuals who emigrated in the '20s, and by those, like Solzhenitsyn, who criticised Russia from within. There have been countless religious emigré publications emphasising the mystical element inherent in Russian communism, and its affinities with Dostoevsky and European existentialism.

Aside from religion, the other important focus for dissent in the Soviet Union is art. Many people who choose to express themselves through art find the straight-jacket of Soviet socialist realism too restricting and are sickened by the wheeling and dealing of the official art world. Tat'yana Mamonova worked in a laboratory and studied pharmacy for a time, painting and writing in her spare moments. She then got a job translating and reviewing for an official journal *Avrora* and used her connections to try and publish her poetry through the legal channels. Eventually she despaired of establishment culture and made contact with dissident artists. Another of the editors of the Almanach, Yuliya Okulova (who writes under the name Voznesenskaya), despite praise and promises from the authorities, has been ignored by the official publishing houses and has come to rely on the dissident artists – the 'non-conformists' – for support and an audience. She has helped arrange unofficial art exhibi-tions, poetry readings and publications, and her own writing, passed in manuscript form from friend to friend, is well known to readers of samizdat.

The cultural underground is not large and the different circles overlap. Tat'yana Goricheva and Natal'ya Malakhovskaya were both philosophy students at Leningrad university in the early '70s and pre-sumably became friends then. Both Tat'yana Goricheva and Yuliya Voznesenskaya took part in a small demonstration held in 1975 to

9

commemorate the 150th anniversary of the Decembrists, the 'first Russian dissidents', and were taken away together by the KGB for questioning.

There has been little about the previous intellectual, artistic or political activity of these women that is explicitly feminist. It is hardly surprising that feminism has not been given the space to develop within the democratic movement, as most dissidents don't analyse Soviet society in a way that would expose the fact that it is founded on the oppression of women – or on national oppression, or the lack of workers' rights. Even within the limited framework of 'human rights', although the dissidents demand that the Soviet Union respect its own constitution they don't, for example, extend this to women and demand that women's right to equal pay, enshrined in the Constitution, be respected too. In a curious echo of the early programmes of the Bolshevik party, dissidents maintain that civil rights must come first: women's rights will then naturally follow. With a perspective like this, to fight for the rights of any individual group would be divisive. Nationalist movements sensitive to the oppression of ethnic minorities, have not proved sympathetic to women's rights either. They see women in romantic terms – the mother of the nation, the purveyor of national culture – and they use the criterion of 'respect for women' as another thing which differentiates them from the Russians. The dissident movement in the Soviet Union has not acknowledged the existence of a 'woman question', still less taken it up.

Though the women have more or less accepted up till now these priorities, their personal lives have been handicapped not only by the lack of civil rights and the curbs on artistic expression, but by the 'dual burden' which they as wives and mothers have shouldered. Tat'yana Mamonova and Yuliya Voznesenskaya have two children each; Natal'ya Malakhovskaya one son; R. Balatova and V. Golubeva are both mothers. One of their bitterest criticisms of Soviet society is that it forces women to choose between motherhood and artistic self-expression. They do not explain in the Almanach how they became aware that their problems are shared and how they gained the confidence to put their ideas into print. An autobiographical essay by Tat'yana Mamonova, published in France[5], indicates that she at any rate has been mulling over the relationship between the democratic movement and feminism for a number of years and that her increasing involvement with the non-conformists was paralleled by a growing resentment at the social inequalities women suffered. In 1970, she submitted an article on sexuality and sex roles – expressing a positive attitude to masturbation and homosexuality – to the glossy magazine *Soviet Women*, which not surprisingly returned it as quite unsuitable for publication. There was no women's movement to which she could turn to discuss her feminism and the dissidents made fun of her ideas. She became more and more convinced that the sexist attitudes which permeate the underground culture prevented women from developing as artists. Women were not treated seriously, they were used sexually. She was particularly angry at the tragic death of a young Leningrad poet, Tanya Kerner, who became pregnant by one of the editors of a leading samizdat journal, decided against an abortion after another male dissident had lectured her on the joys of motherhood and then was left by one and all to look after the child alone. Torn between responsibility to her baby daughter and an overriding love of art, she saw suicide as the only solution. It was only after she had taken her own life that the dissidents appreciated just how good her poetry was.

Working out their relationship with the democratic movement will no doubt be a long and painful process. In the Almanach itself, apart from an oblique reference in the introduction – which criticises those who think that a women's movement is diversionary and argues that women must organise – the authors avoid the issue altogether. The Almanach is addressed not to dissidents, or to women dissidents, or to women artists, or even to women of the intelligentsia; it is addressed to women.

The editorial collective with their city culture, higher education and artistic interests are cut off from some of the experiences of women of other social groups – rural and working class women, women of other nationalities – and their alienation from this other experience sometimes shows in their writing. Nevertheless, they are aware of the problem and the introduction to the Almanach and the article by R. Balatova describes perceptively the way the society and the state divide women against each other. And their main feminist message – that women should have control over their lives – cuts across these social barriers. The major themes of *Women and Russia* – the brutishness of men and the difficulties associated with having and bringing up children – would strike a chord of recognition in the minds of Soviet women, whatever their social background.

The Almanach's feminism is not homogeneous; the women are not unanimous in the solutions they suggest. While most appear to favour some radical change in society's understanding of sex roles or at the very least a more equal division of family responsibilities, some articles hint at a conservative image of women's place. Tat'yana Goricheva understands the ideal of chastity to mean women realising the glory of the traditional female role. In a commentary on the Almanach, subsequently smuggled out to France, with some supplementary articles, she explains its "profoundly negative" tone as a reflection of the early stage of women's revolt. This emotional rejection of the status quo will be followed, she predicts, by an attempt to build a female culture away from men and then the third and highest stage is reached – a reconciliation with the female essence and social role. Hence she is most critical of Zhanna Ivina's contribution to the Almanach, *The Grandeur of Homer and the Purity of Sappho*, which suggests that masculinity and femininity are social constructs.

The differences may become significant in the future. For the moment the women are more concerned with framing the questions than with drawing up clear-cut answers. The differences expressed serve to underline their belief in the right to hold and voice one's own opinions, in the freedom of speech and the press. Feminism is so new; so much needs to be sorted out and discussed. The Almanach's stated aim is to provide a

11

forum for this debate.

The KGB has other ideas. During November 1979, when the Almanach was being put together, Tat'yana Goricheva and Tat'yana Mamonova were called in for questioning. No charges were made, but they were given to understand that if a second issue was produced, they would be arrested. One of the collective, Yuliya Voznesenskaya already knows what the Soviet penal system is like. Exiled to the Siberian town of Irkutsk for five years – her crime was to have circulated her own poetry – she was sentenced to two years in a camp for having returned illegally to Leningrad. It was in prisons on the way to Vorkuta that she witnessed the cruel treatment of women prisoners described by her in the Almanach and other samizdat journals. Unwilling to lay themselves open to such humiliations, the editors of *Woman and Russia* agreed to call off plans for further issues. Though the women have been left at liberty, the authorities have done all they can to make their life unbearable. They can't get work, their letters go astray, their phones are cut off, their neighbours (many of the women live in communal flats) jibe. Yuliya Voznesenskaya has now emigrated to the West and Tat'yana Mamonova has made an official application to do so.

The question for feminists in the West is how we can best support our Soviet sisters. Organising defence activity is not easy. The repression in the Soviet Union and the distances involved make it hard for us to visit these women, or even keep in contact. It is difficult to know how best to express our solidarity. Feminists in this country have been slow to take up international issues, and particularly reluctant to speak out on Eastern Europe. Perhaps one reason for this lack of interest is that criticism of Eastern Europe has nearly always come from the right, and most feminists are unwilling to be associated with Cold War anti-communism. The analyses offered by the left deal almost exclusively in economic categories, and have not helped women find an alternative way of criticising Eastern Europe. The appearance of the Almanach is so exciting precisely because, by giving us a view of Soviet culture and the everyday lives of women there, it opens up the way to a fresh approach.

We hope that feminists who read *Woman and Russia* will want to discuss how the women's movement can build an independent solidarity campaign. The least we can do is seek as much publicity as possible for the Almanach and for the collective of women who produced it. And we also hope that the Almanach, by raising the problems faced by women in Eastern Europe, will provide women in this country with new insights into their own experience and political development.

Women and Eastern Europe Group

Notes

1 The New Economic Policy was introduced to boost the economy after

the devastation of the civil war that followed the revolution. By legalising small-scale private enterprise it allowed a partial return to a market economy. It resulted in massive unemployment (by early 1924 there were nearly 1¼ million unemployed), as well as creating the *Kulak* rich peasant grouping and the *Nepman* (the successful entrepreneur).

2   The average wage in the Soviet Union is 150 roubles a month. It is difficult to give the sterling equivalent because of the different purchasing power of the rouble. Some items such as clothes are relatively more expensive in the USSR while certain goods and services are heavily subsidised by the state. Also living standards are not governed only by money – to acquire certain goods, the right connections are vital.

3   'A Week Like Any Other' was published in – and is still available from – *Spare Rib*, nos 53-59 (1977)

4   The most broadly practised religion has traditionally been Russian Orthodox Christianity.

5   'The New Witch Hunt' in *Rossiyanka* (des femmes: Paris 1980)

АЛЬМАНАХ

ЖЕНЩИНАМ О ЖЕНЩИНАХ
ВЫПУСК 1

10 ДЕКАБРЯ 1979 г

ЭТИ ДОБРЫЕ ПАТРИАРХАЛЬНЫЕ УСТОИ — РЕДАКЦИЯ АЛЬМ.

„РАДУЙСЯ, СЛЕЗ ЕВИНЫХ ИЗБАВЛЕНИЕ" — Т. ГОРИЧЕВА

МАТЕРИНСКАЯ СЕМЬЯ — Н. МАЛАХОВСКАЯ

РОДЫ ЧЕЛОВЕЧЕСКИЕ — Р. БАТАЛОВА

ОБРАТНАЯ СТОРОНА МЕДАЛИ — В. ГОЛУБЕВА

„ЗОЛОТОЕ ДЕТСТВО" — ВАНЯ ПАЗУХИН

ПИСЬМО ИЗ НОВОСИБИРСКА — Ю. ВОЗНЕСЕНСКАЯ

РАСКЛЕЙЩИЦА АФИШ /НОВЕЛЛА/ — И. ТИЩЕНКО

ЛЕТАЮЩИЕ ЯЩЕРЫ /РАССКАЗ/ — С. СОКОЛОВА

ПОЭЗИЯ — Т. МАМОНОВА

МАХАДЕВИ /ПЕРЕВОД/ — Е. ШВАРЦ

„С ГОМЕРОВСКИМ ВЕЛИЧИЕМ И САФИЧЕСКОЙ ЧИСТОТОЙ" —
Ж. ИВИНА

—ВОЗЗВАНИЕ—

ALMANACH
for women about women
number one
10 December 1979

Those good old patriarchal principles — The Editors
"Rejoice, redemption from the tears of Eve" — T. Goricheva
The matriarchal family — N. Malakhovskaya
Human birth — R. Batalova
The other side of the medal — V. Golubeva
"Golden childhood" — Vanya Pazukhin
Letter from Novosibirisk — J. Voznesenskaya
The poster woman/short story/ — I. Tishchenko
Flying lizards/short story/ — S. Sokolova
Poetry — T. Mamonova
Mahadevi/translation/ — E. Shvartz
"With the grandeur of Homer and the purity of Sappho". . .
— Ivina Tallin

— Appeal —

Preamble

How was it brought forth?
In suffering
like a person's birth!
And how was it made beautiful?
Through grief
like a person's face!
How did she get to this place?
Barefoot
as to the town she loves.
And how did she discover it?
With difficulty
as we discover our friends.
So it is she has found you
you who now read these lines!

Those good old patriarchal principles

The Editors

Woman and Russia. We are forced to look at this painful subject by a very real need, at the present time, to vigorously assert the laws of reason. In our century, a world-wide feminization of men and masculinization of women, ie a dislocation of the usual centre of gravity, a re-examination of old attitudes and a re-evaluation of what is important – these are all producing, in Russia, their own specific processes. We intend to clarify these processes. The position of women in society is, currently, a key issue. If in Europe this question is close to being resolved – particularly in France, where four women are in the cabinet and at present a good many women have entered the European parliament – nevertheless, for us this question remains extremely vital. Overall, the mass of women tend to be pessimistic, while men are indifferent, or cynically claim that the problem is insignificant. Although it may be only 'small', it's like the seed from which a forest grows . . .

The pressing problems of life have found us in such a dead-end situation that scepticism is the usual state, the 'norm'. First and foremost this affects women, since they are the most sensitive part of society. In effect the ideal, born in the glorious patriarchal past, of the obedient wife, the uncomplaining mother, the angel of the household hearth – no longer exists. But traditional structure and sluggish consciousness make women into the Caryatids[1] of their home, or more likely, their communal flat.[2] A woman is not in the position to turn aside any inhuman force against her; if she liberates her hands, her home crashes down. However, the myth of a woman's 'weakness' is incredibly tenacious. As a result, a woman venturing beyond the boundaries of her home needs must pay for it. Because women are obliged to participate in socially useful work, as well as do housework (which is still blithely dubbed 'women's work'), it is understandable that such an overburdening makes women frustrated, and subsequently turns them into second-class citizens. Cultivated within patriarchal society there is indeed a notion of equality, to which lip-service is paid. But in the matter of concrete rights, women are called

21

pretentious. Men, fearing competition (especially in relation to highly-placed posts, by which they obviously control women) and dreading the loss of prestige attached to leadership, eulogize the one-sided role of wife and mother. These Pharisees – as if they hadn't noticed that it's women, whom they've bought, that are pulling the wagon on which they sit in state. In the fever of life's non-stop conveyor, the hidden suppression of women's personalities goes on. The slave mentality has not disappeared, rather it has acquired a distorted expression, a more concealed, mis-shapen form. Degrading conditions in maternity homes, abortion clinics and communal flats hinder the development of human self-respect. Men make the standards, but women are judged by society and forced to judge themselves according to how much like men they are. The basic error in such a perception of women demands from them ever newer sacrifices, although they still await sacrifices from society. For the so-called woman question is the most important part of the general struggle for a restructuring of society. You can't deny that women's cultural lot has improved. Nevertheless, they have remained in their former antediluvian conditions of existence. Not token emancipation, but real liberation, is the most important social demand of the times. It is essential to define the specifics of women's position within the family and in production. This is necessary so that women don't, at the cost of indescribable sacrifice, combine two jobs – domestic labour and social labour – but rather that ultimately they can take their place as individuals, enjoying full rights.

Long ago the patriarchy degenerated into a phallocracy. It's under-standable why educated women seek an individual solution and find it in a rejection of childbirth. Intelligent motherhood cannot spring up on barren soil. Female protest against the arbitrary rule of men finds expression not only in a rejection of motherhood, but more often, in a paradoxical rejection of self. This sort of absurd escape is only to be expected, for there is a negative value attached to all things female – for instance the hidden sexist positions in the press. Non-conformists, alas, do not surmount women's usual position. A distorted (ie limited) perception of a woman leads to her being seen as completely worthless, right down to the lower layers of society, where the age-old patience of women has already become pathological, and the unrestrained drunkenness of men has turned them into beasts. Feudal conditions and fatherlessness also exist in intellectual families. In this environment, though, competition occurs more often: who's doing what to whom.[3] It's the conflict of egos. In this instance women, like men, deal with lofty concerns, smoke, drink and swear like men. Women of the intelligentsia don't want to be discriminated against, but male culture tears women apart, implanting a hatred of women (incidentally, there's no concept of 'hatred of men'). The cruel pressure on women of this phallocratic 'culture' crushes any sort of female core in women, and pushes them also towards a hatred of other women. This nonsense flourishes ever more rampantly amongst us. Women, deprived of correct information, full of false doctrines, don't see their real enemy, and running away from themselves, knock into the dark corners of a culture alien to them.

Women's disdain for each other furthers the disintegration of the family, causes an even greater alienation of one sex from the other, and separates women off from each other. Such a low level of self-consciousness reflects the inner conflicts of our society. The past experience of the female half of humanity is not taken into account, and a new experience has not yet been created. Maximum development of intellectual potential leads women into isolation, as it has done in the past. For men the tradition is that women must sacrifice themselves so that men can develop their individuality.

In a country as enormous as this one, parts of which are desolate and run-down, it is difficult to trace all the minutiae of degradation. Minor exposees rarely go further than the columns of newspapers. Undermining new ideas starts right at the grass-roots level, and the voice of justice is barely heard amidst the main clamour. We're always talking about military defence but before defending anyone we've got to assure the vitality of society in and of itself. That means that woman, the giver of life, should come first, and *then* her defenders – not the other way round! In order to make the rights of women equal in reality, society should pay women more than men, not less. Maxim Gorky suggested that for each child a woman should have five years added on to her service record.[4] There have been repeated suggestions to give women meaningful benefit for each child. One ought to realise that Soviet Russia, in its own best exponents, has found a correct, objective solution to the 'woman question'. Lenin never overlooked women when appealing to the masses. A demand for equality for all people could not exclude half the human race. The revolution brought about not only bloodshed, but also a change for the better for the nation (and for individuals). The enthusiasm in Russia during the 1920s is well-known and can be understood. There was full-blooded hope in the new times, new personal relationships and a new family. The Russian revolution resounded throughout the world, and the world was transformed by it. The liberalisation of society as a whole has gradually liberalised the position of women. In Russia this process ground to a halt with the cult of the personality under Stalin. World War II revealed the unbelievable courage of women, capable, as it turned out, not only of giving life, or nurturing, but also of fighting (against fascism). Then there was the period of reconstruction of the country and finally the onset of the thaw (after de-Stalinization) in the 1960s. That was when the 'iron curtain' was rent asunder, when Furtseva[5] the weaver entered the government and Tereshkova[6] flew in space. It would be possible for us to go further (for it's well-known that a society determines the position of the women in it). But . . . Margaret Thatcher, the present Prime Minister in Great Britain, is the logical result of the experiences of Indira Gandhi, Siramovo Bandaranike and other women in the governments of various countries. Although in those countries there is some talk about the dangers of a 'multi-vaginal tyranny', nevertheless, they take the risk. (Here at home in

Literaturnaia Gazeta,[7] for instance, a new trend is described in articles like the one entitled "Are the men really afraid?") And, anyway, taking risks is an honourable thing. Amusingly, but predictably, the Hungarian writer Morits writes about this: "If women take power into their own hands, only then will we understand what decisiveness really is . . . no sentimentality, no fooling about, only women will be able to talk like that with other women." So it seems that they fear the power of women, yet at the same time hope in it. Inside men exists a potential for the innate altruism found in women, but that potential is alienated by the stereotype foisted on us by the patriarchy. Some people are afraid of ridicule, supposedly because the women's movement has been compromised – hasn't the act of giving birth been compromised, and yet people are still being born? Hasn't the church been compromised? Nevertheless the charm of Christ's sermons finds ever new followers . . . Others fear the narrowness of the women's movement, asserting that men also suffer, they say one should not only be interested in women's problems. But surely a gynaecologist isn't judged because he just treats female illnesses, for that is to deny, foolishly, their specific character. Others say that the women's movement is too contrived, that, of course, there are imperfections at this point in time, but when we have established communism, all questions, even the women's question, will just fade away by themselves. Still others fall into the extreme position which accuses the leaders of the women's movement of muck raking.

All the same, this movement, the focus of the most topical ideas around at the moment, is growing. And the stony indifference of the majority of men to it merely encourages its rapid growth. Men, who are destroying themselves with wine, cigarettes and sexual excesses, raise a hue and cry around the subject "Take care of men". At the same time, however, men calmly watch as women pave the streets or move sleepers on the railway. Placidly men listen to the all-pervasive cursing,[8] which undeniably discriminates against women on the level of language. It wouldn't occur to any man to curse the bread with which he is fed, but it's considered in order that women, the creators of life, should be debased by the most vile obscenities. The conservatism of this mass of alcoholics, degenerated to the utmost, the unheeding malevolence towards women of this stunted one-celled organism, this gigantic, spineless amœba – that is the cruel brake to social progress!

editorial staff of the almanach
"Woman & Russia"

Notes

1   These were pillars, sculpted in the form of a woman, and used to hold up Greek temples.
2   Communal flats are not 'communal' in our understanding of the word, ie people do not come together in any sort of voluntary or collective

way, nor do they share food or services. What it means, usually, is several families occupying a large flat, each family to one of the rooms in it, and everyone sharing the kitchen, bath and loo.

3 Who's doing what to whom – the title of an article by Lenin.

4 Working people accumulate points for so many years of work, thus a service record.

5 Furtseva was a weaver, and became Minister of Culture in 1960.

6 Tereshkova was the first woman cosmonaut; in 1963 she flew into space.

7 *Literaturnaia Gazeta* is a weekly newspaper and besides reporting run-of-the-mill stuff, like party congress news, or visits of delegations from other socialist countries, it has very interesting discussions on its pages about problems of daily life: relations between the sexes, whither the family, alcoholism, juvenile delinquency, and much more.

8 Some of the worst obscenities in the Russian language are based on the word for mother.

"Rejoice, redemption from the tears of Eve"

T. Goricheva

Beloved sister,

On the day of the Assumption of Our Lady[1] I want to write to you about the meaning the Mother of God has for my life and how through her I was able to find myself and my God.

I could never hope to tell you of all the gifts bestowed on those who pray to Her and contemplate Her, of the daily revelation of Love and Sacrifice. But I would like to say a few words about the Mother of God as the perfect incarnation of humanity and of women. The Mother of God is womanhood itself. She lifts the curse placed by earlier religions on everything 'female'. The goddess Astarte was the counterpart of Yahweh. The Great Mother figures of pagan religion were the embodiment of irrationality, superstition and sensuality. Christianity was and still is the only religion to deify the flesh. Christianity alone has conquered the dualism of body and spirit. God has appeared on earth in bodily form and Christians believe that they will live after death in the flesh as well as in the spirit. Thus there is complete interdependence of body and mind. That is why secret desires are no less real and material than manifest sin and punished likewise: " . . . whosoever looketh on a woman to lust after her . . ."[2]

The purity of the Mother of God raises her above the Angels. She is the "most chaste", She is the Church of Christ, She is "most beautiful".

From childhood the Mother of God knew neither worldly nor physical lust. Nothing that was unclean dared approach Her. For the first time in the history of humanity, corporal and intuitive elements are fused harmoniously. The female essence, utterly debased and degraded by pagan religion, is illuminated so brightly and raised to such lofty heights that it becomes a vessel for the perception of the Holy Spirit. "And Thy womb is wider than the heavens." Rejoice you who are a Temple endowed by the Holy Spirit.

All this became clear to me as my spirit recovered and I found the church.

St Augustine said that Christ is the solution to all problems. One could say the same of the Most Holy Queen, the ideal Human Being, the ideal woman.

What problems did I solve as I trod the path of self knowledge, and began to contemplate Her and pray to Her every day?

The problem is self-realisation.

Seven years ago, you remember, we read Karl Jung on the two archetypes of female consciousness. Some women, he said, identify with their mothers; others rebel against them.

The young girl who has a strong 'Electra complex' is jealous of her father's relationship with her mother and from early childhood expresses anti-mother, anti-woman attitudes. Her super ego adopts male virtues and standards. She develops her intellect and her will; possibly she shows contempt for the flesh (and for motherhood as a part of the material world) and inclines towards spiritualism. Such women are unwilling to enter into marriage or to have children. They contribute to culture and science, sometimes they become religious 'fanatics', sometimes politicians. But they may also turn into criminals, anarchists, prostitutes – bearers of the forces of destruction.

I admitted to you then that I felt myself to be in the power of this second archetype.

But it was not only the 'archetype' that was to blame for the fact that I had lost touch with my female self. The whole Soviet educational system aims at developing an abstract, one-dimensional, 'pseudo-male' personality.

Whom did we imitate, you and me, at our school benches? What idols did we have? We admired Pechorin, Onegin[3] and the other romantic heroes of literature whose intellect and inner tragedies raised them above the crowd and made them interesting. And, of course, none of us wanted to be like the silly Princess Mary[4], or any of those other women who were deceived and deserted, who knew nothing of the spiritual life and served only as fodder for the author's plot.

And what did we know about marriage? We delighted in the romantic enthusiasms of Natasha Rostova[5] and were puzzled by the "yellow nappies" of the epilogue. We knew that the only interesting marriages are the unhappy ones (for "all families are happy in the same way"[6]) and no one wanted to be like Afanasiya Nikitichna and Pulkheriya Ivanovna.[7] In a word, we acquired romantically unreal and morbid ideas about love and developed a revulsion towards marriage.

When we were at school, did we have any inkling that a woman has a path in life, which while equal to the path of a man is different and special? How could we, when they taught us to honour the intellect (more precisely, to honour reason) and spurn the heart; school and life spoke with one voice and told us that the most important thing was to be in control and not controlled by others, to be the master of our own destiny. Sacrifice (throughout the ages, one of the highest and most important ideas) we could only think of as something 'passive' and people who were the victims of their own insignificance and weakness, were for us, worthy only of pity. Some of us, it is true, were prepared to make sacrifices, but only for the sake of some high ideal which always remained pale, abstract and distant.

We left school with this distorted vision of human nature and of ourselves; we held all 'women's' duties (cooking, washing, bringing up children – how boring and commonplace) in absolute contempt.

Maybe you will ask why it is I am talking of the degradation of the female essence, when woman in our country is emancipated to the hilt, enjoys equal rights with man and occupies all key social positions in fact and not just in words?

I am sure that someone has already answered your question and explained that it is not woman who is emancipated, but man who is 'feminised'. In a society like ours, a man is incapable of being independent and of consciously building his own life. Woman is the leading force, both in the family (which is being destroyed by drink) and at work. These days, women are the Jill-of-all-trades; they are monstrously overburdened. They are the modern martyrs. I'm sure you must have heard what a stir that short story describing the daily life of a Soviet woman and published officially in the journal, *New World*, created in the West.[8] In a society which flouts and tramples on everything that is sacred, the strengths and talents of people are perverted and human nature itself distorted. The crude unspirituality of the dominant values produces an undifferentiated one-dimensional man, a sexless, 'homo sovieticus'. What happened to us after school, you know already: romantic love, hasty marriage, endless nagging, disappointment, high-handed separations etc.

In the 'pre-Christian' years that followed, my female self suffered even greater humiliations. Relegated to the unconscious it took its own revenge, encouraging me to live according to the desperate principle that 'nothing is forbidden', to live a life of folly, promiscuity and existential rebellion which made loving anyone an impossibility and led only to the steady dissipation of mind and body. Though I had banished my female self from my consciousness (along with all the 'conventions'), its power over me did not abate. Rather it assumed a sinister, demonic form; it became an underground Dionysian force. I thought that my life was ruled by my 'sharp intellect' but in reality I was the slave of my unconscious. Thus our dissolute 'paganism' induced us to reject our female essence, just as the pagan religion of the past had done. We saw the female essence as the vehicle of irrational and demonic forces and were frightened by its chaos and violence.

And then She appeared, rescuer of the fallen. Rejoice, the Daughter, Our Saviour.

Prayer to the Most Holy Queen helped me to discover and resurrect my female self in all its purity and absoluteness.

I understood for the first time the spiritual meaning of chastity, the most important of all virtues. Before I had always talked about chastity in order to ridicule it: chastity was something old-fashioned, an indication of naive ignorance or cheap provincialism. The word shone and glowed with deep meaning and held out the promise of a wise and whole person. But at that time such a person was beyond our comprehension.

The Mother of God took the path of chastity. Her followers are not only those who take holy orders, but those who live in Christian marriage.

Just as the new Adam has redeemed the sins of the old, so the new Eve has lifted the curse from the old Eve to become the symbol of the Church.

Humanity finds justification in the Mother of God and so likewise does the female essence.

We find in Her the image of the perfect Human Being. In the first place She has conquered all internal duality. She is the 'full' and whole person. Her completeness is said to "be wider than the heavens".

But as we know, in the humdrum of everyday life, fullness and wholeness are more often than not held in suspicion and equated with reticence, stagnation and death.

With the Mother of God it is quite otherwise. She is all-giving. She listens. Of her it is written: "Blessed are those who listen". The Most Holy Queen is a model of self-abnegation. In all things She obeys the will of God whose word "is written in her heart".

Consequently, She combines the perfect fullness of life with the willingness to sacrifice all for God. That is why she is called the proto-type of the Church.

Prayer to Her illuminates the whole depth of the unconscious, gives believers self-understanding, keeps their faith strong, compelling them to transcend themselves in obedience to the Divine.

The Bearer of God is the depth which leads to the heights. Rejoice, Ye heights, impenetrable to the human mind. Rejoice, Ye depths, invisible even to the eyes of Angels. We shall pray to Her, sister, that she may not abandon us in our misery.

Rejoice, zealous Champion of the Christian world.

This letter is only the beginning. I have said nothing so far about the 'eschatological newness' connected with Her birth, or about the Mother of God as the Pillar of Maidenhood and as the Church. But God willing I shall do this in my next letter.

Lord Jesus Christ, save us through our prayers to your most Chaste Mother.

Notes to "Rejoice . . ."

1   August 15
2   Matthew ch 5, verse 28
3   Pechorin and Onegin are the two most famous heroes of early 19th century Russian Romantic literature. Pechorin is the 'Hero of our Time', in the novel by Mikhail Lermontov, and Onegin is the main character of Pushkin's poem 'Evgenii Onegin'. Both are 'superfluous

men' in the Byronic tradition, wealthy, cynical and bored, they travel the world in search of experience powerful enough to arouse their emotions and give their life meaning and purpose.

4 Princess Mary is loved and left by Pechorin.

5 Natasha Rostova is the heroine of Leo Tolstoy's *War and Peace*.

6 This is from the opening sentence of Tolstoy's novel, *Anna Karenina*.

7 Afanasiya Nikitichna and Pulkheriya Ivanovna appear in a short story by Nikolai Gogol, 'Old-fashioned Landowners'. They and their husbands live in a provincial back-water, are quiet, polite and pleasant and spend most of their time eating.

8 The 'short story' referred to is 'A Week Like Any Other', by Natal'ya Baranskaya, published in the Soviet journal, *New World* in 1969 (no 11) and serialised in *Spare Rib* (nos 53-59, 1977).

The matriarchal family

N. Malakhovskaya

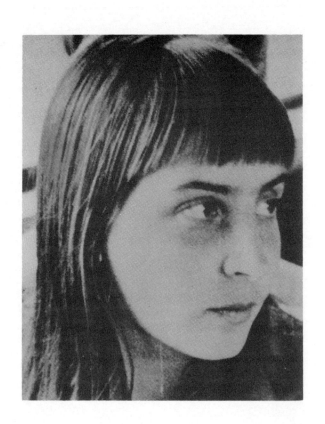

Why is it today that women are in such an unbearably difficult position? Let us try to trace how the position of women has changed over the different stages of historical development.

The division of labour between men and women took place in the depths of the past, when human society was just beginning. At this time it was not only natural but also progressive. The hunting of mammoths and the protection of the species from predators could not be done by the same person who reproduced the life of the species. And because women performed the labour of reproducing the species, a labour of the most difficult and dangerous kind, the 'light' women's work which is spoken of with so much contempt today was allocated to them, not to men. A wild beast might tear a man to pieces: in which case he suffered the same pain as a woman giving birth, and like her he risked his life. There was thus a *balance of pain, a balance of risk and a balance of labour*.

Centuries passed, society developed, changed internally. Patriarchy was in its prime. The need to defend the life of the species from wild beasts vanished; hunting ceased to be the chief source of food; risk, pain and heavy labour were no longer essential elements of the life of a man. But neither the risk, nor the pain nor the heavy labour could possibly disappear from the life of a woman – or humanity would have ceased to exist. However, this was somehow forgotten, pushed into the background. Birth was no longer "the miracle of the coming of a person into the world", but something that happened as a matter of course, a free service, providing a labour force for the workshops, factories and armies.

What were the different responsibilities of men and women in this period? In most families the woman brought up the children and ran the household, while the man earned money to support the whole family and in poorer families did 'men's work' around the house (chopped wood, fetched water, did repairs). In this way, the balance of risk and pain disappeared, and only the balance of labour remained (we could point to the exemplary Ul'yanov family[1], where the mother devoted herself entirely to bringing up her six children). The inequality of political, legal and other rights made itself felt. And also, we mustn't forget, there was the social inequality: in this period, some women worked in the factories or as hired farm labourers, while the others had no responsibilities except that of reproducing the species. The harshness of women's lives was perceived in the context of general social inequality and solutions were proposed within these terms. Lenin's words, "From now on cooks will take part in running the state", summed up the beautiful dream of the new family, a great hope of new relations between the sexes. But during the period of the Stalin cult, the question of the family was declared to be secondary, which meant in reality, that it was completely ignored.

Today, women are formally liberated and have equal political and legal rights (or wrongs) with men – but they do not have moral equality. As far as responsibilities are concerned, there is no equality at all.

No one has freed men from the responsibility of supporting a family, but rising prices and the greatly increasing cost of living have meant that the money men earn isn't enough even for a family of three. According to the official figures, the average wage in the USSR is 150 roubles (a month), a sum on which three people could survive only by half-starving, by totally depriving the child of the vegetables and fruit which are essential, and by ceasing even to think about spending money on clothes (which we have to do in our severe climate). But this is just an average, and the official average at that. Many men are content to work for less (often this is connected with the wish to work in their chosen field – as a rule, professional people earn less than workers).

And if we take a step closer to reality and recall what percentage of their earnings men squander on drink, we see that they have completely forgotten that it is their duty to feed their children.

So that's how seriously men take their most important responsibility. As far as men's work around the house is concerned, in the town at least, it has practically vanished with the introduction of central heating, running water and gas. The man feels that he is above household chores. The man who even knows how to 'knock a nail in' is a biological rarity today. All 'nails' needed in the household are today 'knocked in' by the woman. And the men who do 'help' women in their 'light work' stand out in the crowd and can be counted on one's fingers, so there's no sense in taking them into consideration.

Thus there exist today, to put it crudely, two ways of life for men:
1   After work the man goes drinking and then tumbles into bed or kicks up a row;
2   After work the man sprawls on the sofa with the paper or sits in front of the television. (Maybe there's also the ideal man who occupies himself after work with a hobby or some sort of creative activity.)

Anyway, we'll stop at these two, which are enough to show us that men today do not carry out even one function – they do not even support their own family. Now let us count up the responsibilities that women have:

1   As in the past, we create the future generations with our own blood and pain. If today all women refused this mortally dangerous labour, there would be no one left on earth; the human race would die out, there would be no future generations to benefit from our experience and the culture we have created. However, women don't get just rewards for their labour. The child who cuts a finger gets more sympathy than a woman dying from pain in the agony of giving birth. Nowhere is the human individual so trampled upon as in a maternity home, even in the best. The pregnant woman is regarded with disgust and contempt, as if she were a loose woman; her agony is looked on as proof of her own special degradation. The woman who decides to brave it out for the sake of bringing a new person into the world meets only with rudeness and humiliation. She is treated like a dumb animal who has no control over her own actions.

The incredible filth which you find in maternity homes increases the physical sufferings of women, and the categorical ban on the admission of relatives intensifies her mental sufferings. Husbands, who don't have a clue what their wives have to go through, cannot treat them with proper respect. These men who haven't spilt a drop of blood to have a child, will a week later turn on the young mother with the same old endearments: "Give that here, you idiot"; "Do this, you fool."

2   Woman's 'light' work is not at all light these days. Even in large towns there's little to buy in the shops and what there is won't make a good meal. Since the average family doesn't have the money to buy a fridge, most women have to run round the shops every day. Poor supplies lead to huge queues for vegetables, fruit and other scarce items. A loving mother is forced to spend hours, even whole days, standing in queues. However hard you look, you won't find any men in there, although the queues of men in front of beer shops never get any shorter. And the rise in prices and the fall in quality of goods make our position completely hopeless: since, besides the responsibility of finding ways and means to feed our family under such conditions, we've got other responsibilities.

3   We have to bring up our children, for nurseries and kindergartens are *utopias*, which have turned out in reality to be anti-utopias – you entrust healthy children to these institutions and they come home sick and tired. A woman constantly has to get sick notes and take time off to stay home with her child – only not with a healthy child as in the past, but with a sick one.

4   And yet at the same time she has to earn money, and not in order to better her material situation, but simply so as not to die of hunger. And this places her in an *unnatural* position. People don't like to employ a woman with children and at the interview they always show a preference for men. If a woman gets a job, they turn against her after the first sick note. The unfortunate mother turns out, as always, to be *herself* to blame for the fact that her child is ill! They say, "You had the child, you have to take the consequences!" and move her to a lower paid job. After the second or third sick note, they find ways of getting rid of her.

Thus the 'ratio' of responsibilities between men and women today is one to four. But there are families where this disproportion is intensified as a result of particular individual circumstances. It's rare to make a living out of the arts, or even make a bit of extra money. If you devote yourself to the arts, your labours are unpaid. And if you're a woman? If art becomes your fifth job?

In the present circumstances, it is in practice impossible to reconcile being a mother and an artist (if you don't count the rare instances where the grandmother takes on the whole responsibility for the children). When she has a baby, a woman has to give herself up as a bad job. I know women who say almost with pride, "Now I am not myself, now I am my child". And bit by bit, the life of the woman is exchanged for the life of the child. The family is built on the bones of women, on their blood and tears. The family destroys the artist in women. Nowhere will you find a family where the man, even the most untalented, will do for a woman what a woman, even the most talented, does for her husband. No man will sacrifice his artistic potential so that she can develop her abilities. The woman says, "Your ambitions are mine", and kills the Mozart inside her. If she doesn't do it herself, her husband does it for her. Or, what's most likely – he says to his wife, "There's never been and cannot be a female Mozart, the Lord God didn't create you for that".

Men think that only they are capable of creating cultural values. But the culture they've created won't do for us. We can see that it tangibly lacks something, and that what it lacks is love – that same love which men hypocritically hide behind and sell on every street corner.

Love bursts from your heart, tears you apart, it's a mortal sin to stifle it, not to give it life. To become an artist, a woman must make efforts unknown to men, heroic efforts. But she will do this, in order to create a new culture which will transform life.

And finally, we come to the last question: the moral rights of women. The family, the same which destroys the artist in woman, is also all too often founded on the denial of her love. Women today, as in the past (with the exception of the Rennaissance period), have only the *right of refusal* but not the *right of choice* in love. They are not free to choose whom they will love; they can choose only from those who have already chosen them. Unrequited love is a torment, but it is a hundred times more of a torment for women who not only do not have the right to make their feelings known to the one they love, but will be put to shame if those around them even guess at their feelings. (It is obvious that this reflects, as well as everything else, the one-sided male view of love which prevails in our society: the man assumes that when a woman says "I love you" she means the lust which is all he himself is capable of feeling and he therefore sees something indecent in her admission.) At the same time, the man has the right not only to tell any woman he loves her, but also to use all means, even blackmail, to ensure that his desire is satisfied.

Men's attitude to love contains, with rare exceptions, an element of pure brutality: surely by despising the woman he loves, a man shames himself as well – he who only yesterday confessed his love to her. The fact that men don't even notice this contradiction is all the more distressing: it means that even when they wept and fell on their knees, somewhere in the depths of their soul they were conscious of the temporary and flippant nature of their oath. The initial lack of seriousness in the attitude to love and the family is the fault from which real vices quickly develop. The man refuses unpleasant family responsibilities – so what, it's his right! He tries as far as possible to spend his wages on himself, and leaves far too little to feed or dress his children properly. And this is also his right. He goes from woman to woman, no one blames him for this, no one brands him with the title women earn if they behave in that way. He is free, everything is fine . . .

But men have not noticed that a *matriarchal family* is appearing, has in fact already appeared. That women, regardless of their education, their social and material position, are trying to get rid of their drunkard-husbands. That where a man hasn't yet been driven out of the family, he has lost, together with his responsibilities, all of his rights, including the chief of them – the right to bring up his children, the right to their love, the right to have a direct influence on the future generation. Men are only producers, not fathers. Usually the family breaks up not because of a new love taking the place of the old, but because the children ask their mother to take them away from their father.

Everything is still easy and pleasant for men, but their position is getting a little uncomfortable. Unconsciously, they already sense their inferiority, their loss, some sort of inadequacy. Human society, the society of mothers and children, is separating itself from them. Their freedom hangs over them – like the sword of Damocles. And the children who have been brought up by another sort of person will never take their prodigal father back. They will create another life in which there will be no place for paternal brutishness.

So what is the position of woman today? She has to become everything, *so she is becoming everything*. Life itself is turning the heaviest of her responsibilities into rights, and the more tormenting the responsibilities, the fuller, the more undivided her rights. The latest poet of patriarchy dreams in vain that:

"Woman will be a woman
a mother, a sister and wife,
she'll tuck you up and she'll wake you
and smooth the path of your life
her husband and son she will follow
to the very ends of the earth . . ."

Women who have not known male support will never agree to become the appendage of a man, to be only a mother, only a wife, only a sister. Women have more serious things to be doing than "tucking up" drunken men and waking them up again. And anyway, these days it is women more often than men who travel "to the very ends of the earth".

So women survive the living death devised by man and nature. With boundless courage they shoulder all responsibility, and with their bodies and their souls, they forge the future.

Human birth

R. Batalova

I would agree to stand in battle many times
Rather than once experience the pangs of giving birth.
(Euripedes, *Medea*)

This nightmare has not ended. It will never end now. It has remained in you. As the glaring offence remains, when horror dies away and death grows cold. This is more terrible than death because you continue to feel. You have died, but you feel pain. You are exhausted, but it still torments you. You didn't know how to scream, you were ashamed to scream – so you didn't scream, you sobbed like a mortally wounded animal. This was the reality. This was not your frenzied imagination which had frightened you, but had offered something to comfort you. It had scared and soothed. Reality turned out to be inescapable. You might find the door open but there was no way you could run from your burden. Inescapable, it was inside you. You fell into complete dependence on those whom you at first despised – they did stupid crosswords – on those whom you then began to hate – they talked about something else while women cried in terror. They, only they, could offer you an escape. But the escape which you needed was not their escape. They jabbed and jabbed and jabbed you, until your body, your organism, ceased to obey you. It submitted to them, to their needle, thrusting over and over again into your skin. Convulsions forced a howl from your lips, but you could change nothing. Even if you were a genius, you would still be in constant risk of having your personality crushed. To achieve the position of a man, you have (even if you are more talented) to make superhuman efforts, asserting yourself, proving yourself, fighting for your individuality. But even the most worthless man is apriori better than you. If you achieve what he does, your victory is a hundred times greater than his, for at every step you have to overcome obstacles he has no idea of. Even if we leave the psychological aspect aside, your body itself is bombarded by ailments and dangers also unknown to men.

Your body is prematurely worn out in the service of humanity. Of course you can wriggle out of this by denying yourself love and children. You may escape pregnancy, if you can avoid being raped, but then such 'trifles' as menstruation, menopause will still exhaust and destroy you. Destroy both your body and your soul. You can avoid the service of humanity, but not the 'opinion' of society, biased entirely in favour of men. You will become a pariah, a non-person, despised by this society. You go this way or that, but everywhere a punishment has been prepared. If you are not a mother (they give this sacred name the vilest associations), you are either an 'old maid' or a whore. Don't get caught in the labyrinths they have constructed for you – only blind alleys await you there!

You protect yourself from these unendurable burdens and insoluble problems by becoming insensitive. Insults and cares turn you into a stone. The gulf between you and men only widens. They are always right. You, who gave birth to them, are always wrong. Over the years you lose your personality, without ever finding yourself. You are eaten up by a terrible emptiness and tiredness of spirit, which, turning into a violent dissatisfaction with your own life, borders on disgust with life in general. Pregnancy, undoubtedly a parasitic phenomenon, destroys your youth. Your faith. The meaning of your own existence. And all for children, preferably male!

No appeals will bring home to even the best of men your complete lack of any escape, unless society finally abandons the well-worn path of glorious patriarchy. Patriarchy somehow or other always forces women into a cage. Whatever they do for the good of society, staying within the confines of their sex, is just their duty and their obligation. It is even thought that this is all they yearn for ... Whatever men do is a favour on their part, a kindness, a good deed. Women are by nature self-sacrificing – this is normal, they never receive any credit. Whatever pain, whatever suffering a woman manfully (what a word!) endures, it is not her, but the man who is praised, although he didn't lift a finger. The mere fact that by chance he was born a man puts him at once in a privileged position. He can permit himself every physical and moral indulgence. It doesn't matter whether it is athleticism or infantilism. Women are not so much leant on as crushed. Isn't pregnancy a sweet, desirable burden! Men have persuaded not only themselves, but also you of this. And nothing can dissuade them. Not even the permitting of abortion, which has revealed that women will often undergo this unpleasant operation (and without anaesthetic for economy's sake) in order to escape from the joys men offer them. Hypocritically, they go on glorifying motherhood. They present you with this deformity, this sickness, and you are happy to accept their gift, in order to obtain at least some recognition in this hostile society. But you lose a great deal in obtaining it. All this is shrewdly thought out. You are a mother, be proud! – they tell you, but your name is defiled on the street corner, it is used in the vilest obscenities. And this isn't all: look at yourself! You are no longer that fresh flower which your master might wish to pluck. You have withered, and you are reproached for this. You quickly become devalued. You're always the loser. That's how it is. Even when, worn out with suffering, you say to yourself "Let it be a son!" so that he won't experience your agony, your selflessness will not be noticed. Patriarchy places no value on it, for you are *obliged* to bear sons! Then your son despises you, he is taught this so quickly that he doesn't have time to think it out: that it was you who gave him life, it was you who said "Let it be a son!" and freed your child from the terrible burden of being a woman. If you say any of this, you'll soon get an answer: it was nature who decided to give life to a male: "The mother is not the creator of her child" – these lines of genius were written at the very dawn of patriarchy. Thus, patriarchy put you in your place once and for all. And for centuries you have given your blood, your health, your 'useless' life for your sons – intuitively you calculate that at least through your son you can participate in the blessings of the patriarchal world. You may even begin to despise your sex, running down other women and elevating the man you love, or to whom you gave birth, but even this self-denial won't put you on the same level as them, you'll just be doing your bit to prop up patriarchy. Men couldn't care less about your labours. They are separated from you by a thick glass wall, which they rely on to protect them from the noise you occasionally create (in your few spare moments). They are safe from your howls. They are observers, you the sacrifice. They find your plight amusing. Perhaps they allow you to take a few pawns, but they win in the end, since the rules of the game are different for them than for you. They are aware of this, even though they may not consciously think it. Sometimes your voice reaches them behind the glass wall (when you scream too loudly) "Change the world!" "Make the world just!" but men have no reason to change the world. The system is comfortable and profitable for them. They would rather start a new war, which will exterminate your children. They would rather invent a new rocket – a rocket increases their prestige, reinforces their primacy – than take the heavy chains from you. What will they gain from your emancipation? Your liberation will only create inconveniences for them. It is much simpler and more pleasant to take comfort in the thought that there is no need for reform. March 8 (once a year!) they dust the sideboard. They declare 1975 Women's Year and go through the appropriate formalities. Men also want to be known for their altruism and in their better moments behave unselfishly, but this doesn't last. They won't admit to themselves that they trample women underfoot from a feeling of inferiority, envious of your original, genuine altruism. A hypocritical half-measure takes the place of their altruism. They help you (note the verb!) to wash the family dishes or look after the child. They 'help', glowing with awareness of their own unselfishness. You somehow or other (they may refuse, you can't) have got to wash the dishes or look after the child, who has cost you so dear. Like a flapping fish, you are sure to end up in the net of slavery, and men will always have at their disposal a heap of arguments about your inadequacy.

"You carry your stomach as if it was the whole world . . . " You bend under its weight. What awaits you?! You wait as people wait for an earthquake, a catastrophe, you want to forget yourself, feel nothing, but the catastrophe is inevitable. Slow rumblings give way to the explosion. You feel the ground slip under your feet and you curse love. Three sleepless nights, forty-eight hours revulsion from food, continual exhausting contractions – all this tears your body from the power of your reason. Panic-stricken and covered in blood, you writhe in convulsions, run into the corridor in search of someone, but you see the gynaecologists and midwives sitting out shift after shift . . . From your first minute in the *rodilka* (the irreverent name given to this dreadful place, this Golgatha) you freeze with fear. The groans, sobs and pleas of the women in labour would have a traumatic effect on any newcomer. To the question:

"How can you let this happen?" the doctors answer

"The babies must come first.

Women can endure it all . . . "

Ten trestlebeds, on which the unfortunate victims of patriarchy writhe. Bloody sheets. Eyes huge from pain. Bitten lips (they prudently cut your nails on admission). Soaking wet nightgowns. Dishevelled hair.

"Why do we all have to be together?"

"There are so many of you."

"But we are human beings!"

"Forget the philosophy. Lie down and get on with it."

"You're being rude."

"We've got no choice."

"Nonsense, these women need attention and sympathy if anyone does."

"We've got enough work as it is."

You lie down. You shut your eyes tight. You stick your fingers in your ears. For all these groans tear you to pieces. An unbearable sight for a normal mind. Delirium. Horror personified. A nightmare, hanging on a thread of nerves. Bloodstained trestlebeds, in place of corals . . . You clutch your head. You try to plunge yourself into oblivion. The contractions wake you. The contractions return you to this room, to this ceaseless groaning. To reality!

Your stomach is transformed into an alien body. It moves by its own will. It is no longer in your power. You try to contain its jerks with yours hands. You've left your ears free, they can hear again. One cry, then another pierces your brain:

"Doctor, you promised to help me! Doctor!" a skinny girl cries in a broken voice.

"Midwife dear, Klavochka, do come here please!" this is the voice of the woman in the next bed, who you try not to look at.

"I don't want to live, I don't wa-ant to" a voice from the other corner of the ward. A voice which ends in a heartrending shriek.

"Mother, what's it all for?" gasps someone else.

Your heart stops. Your throat dries up. A thought as penetrating as a scream: get out of here! But a new contraction nails you to the bed. Minutes. Hours. Morning comes. The groans pile up on one another. A trail of blood leads from the beds, from the labour to the delivery ward. A trail of blood, which dries before they have time to mop it up. You can lift yourself up and look out of the window. Your time hasn't come yet. There below, through the branches of trees you see another world. You hear carefree laughter . . . They bring in a new patient. She wears glasses and is holding herself with studied calm. In half an hour her glasses fall on the stone floor, she is terrified by what she has seen.

The foul face of patriarchy. Its convulsions. Agony. One of the prophets foretold its rapid demise: "The power of woman will come on Earth".

The other side of the medal

V. Golubeva

To fulfill one's destiny as a mother is the greatest blessing nature holds in store for a woman. Only a woman who has experienced motherhood is capable of understanding, feeling and valuing what a responsibility the life of an infant is: there *is* a point to those 'mother heroine' medals.

But here I want to talk about the woman who is brave enough to have and bring up a child on her own: the single mother. What inspires her to take such a dangerous step? Each of these women has her own reasons, her own complicated and contradictory personal motives, the analysis of which we will leave to her.

Many women decide on this courageous act without realising quite what a thorny path they have chosen. Women, for example, who have no close relatives or even parents who could help out in a crisis.

They shouldn't expect much from society. The state pays out five roubles a month for the maintenance of an illegitimate child, and you only get these five roubles after a whole series of formalities and humiliations. You aren't informed that you're entitled to the money, and they won't send it to you at home. Anyway it's a joke – you couldn't survive for two days on that amount. But a single woman with a child, and with no one to turn to but herself, needs support for at least one year.

Only a woman who has fully thought out and foreseen all the difficulties of being a single mother, and saved up enough money for this, can live comfortably for a year without working. But very few manage this because in practice it's very hard to foresee what's going to happen tomorrow. Yes, and what about those who don't think, don't plan things, those who can't support themselves for a year? What are women supposed to do if they aren't that adaptable, and can't so easily compromise with their conscience?

It's only by making superhuman efforts that they can keep alive themselves and their children, the future members of our society – a society which doesn't take the trouble to consider the real meaning and consequences of its rhetorical slogans about 'women's emancipation'. No one thinks about the price a woman must pay for her so-called freedom, about which so much is said and written, but which doesn't in fact exist.

So a woman brings up her child, and when he is one, she naturally relies on the state, on nurseries. But this presents a new problem: how to get a place. To get a child into a nursery the child has to be on the waiting-list before it's even born. There's only one other solution, and that's to give up your job and go to work in a nursery yourself, for that way they'll take the child too. If you don't have any medical qualifications you'll have to do the dirtiest heaviest work, while making sure that your child is all right. This is a fact of no small importance, because it's a terrible mistake to think that your child will be just as well off in a state institution as at home.

Nurseries and kindergartens are the most dreadful institutions in the nation's health service. The staff in general consists of elderly and middle-aged women, with a small percentage of younger women who have come to work as cleaners for their children's sake. Most of the elderly and middle-aged women no longer have children of their own, and it's difficult to see what brings them to this garden of childlike innocence and purity. It's certainly not a spirit of self-sacrifice and self-denial on behalf of these weak defenceless infants, who need such a great deal of care. They have to be carried around all day long, their noses and hands wiped, and their nappies changed. They need to be spoon-fed. One sister and one nanny will have a group of twenty-five to thirty-five children to look after. How much love and patience one has to have to greet these little charges with a smile every day, to look after them all day and return the following day with fresh spiritual strength!

Most women are incapable of any such thing. Most of them are guided by mercenary considerations. They know that these defenceless little creatures can't tell anyone about what they silently witness, since they're not yet capable of understanding and appraising the behaviour of the adults to whom their lives are entrusted. Some people take advantage of this. I've had dealings myself with these people, and I've never met such cruel and vicious types. They go to work there with the definite intention of stealing the children's food. They mix meat half-and-half with bread, blessing the clever cook who invented such dishes as rissoles, meatballs, dumplings and beefburgers. They dilute sour cream and milk with water – it's not hard to do.

In the summer holidays children are sent out of town to *dachas*[1] (summer cottages) in the country to breathe fresh air, build up their strength and eat fruit and vegetables – and then, too, there's a profit to be made.

The staff of the group divide amongst themselves the fruit parents bring their children, and leave the children with the biscuits, chocolates and other sweet things which are bad for them.

The standards of hygiene are appalling. The little girls are hardly ever washed, and are dried either with their nightgowns or a common towel. Their hands and feet don't get washed very often either, and are dried on the same towel.

I remember the *dacha* at Bengardovka in the summer of 1976. The hospital hut which housed the convalescent children was very over-crowded. Here there were children suffering from serious respiratory diseases with complications, and others with mumps and dysentry. The ambulances knew this route well and called in here almost every day.

After a holiday like this the single woman who has entrusted her child to a state institution can only rack her brains as to where else she can safely leave her child.

The reasons for this state of affairs in our pre-school institutions should be sought in the structure of the health service and the organisation of its workforce. Low wages result in a labour shortage and high staff turn-over. A qualified nurse is paid eighty to ninety roubles a month, a junior nurse seventy-five roubles. The labour of women who are called upon to look after and educate our future generation – and who sacrifice their spiritual health and strength in the process – is seriously undervalued.

In the Soviet Union, though, there is the right to choose. If you can't cope with the burden of having a child, you have the possibility of not having one. Abortion is legal in the Soviet Union. Just ten to fifteen minutes (the time the operation takes) will save you all the trouble and unpleasantness entailed in having a child. But what spiritual and physical agony these dreadful minutes cost! I'm sure that most women who have experienced this inhuman torture but once, would refuse this barbaric operation if they had proper living conditions. Society, however, doesn't seem to understand why a woman has an abortion. Sometimes – although very rarely – when she fills out the numerous forms on her admission to the hospital, a woman is asked why she doesn't want to have the child. The answer is generally the same – bad living conditions or low wages. I don't know where all this information goes, or whether it even goes anywhere at all! In any case, our 'humane' society has done all it can to ensure that in every situation imaginable the 'emancipated' Soviet woman feels the full consequences of her freedom.

If a woman does decide to have an abortion, she has to be prepared literally to go through hell. First come the humiliations she must endure when she goes to the maternity clinic to collect the pile of papers for her impending ordeal. She will be treated there with a blatant lack of interest and even with contempt. The next stages she has to go through to achieve her aim will bring her further humiliations. She has to queue for an appointment. Depressed careworn women sit on benches along the walls of a vast, stuffy, ill-lit hall, waiting there often as long as one-and-a-half to two hours.

Hours pass, her predestined agony draws nearer, and finally she goes in to the abortion clinic. The one on Lermontov Prospekt is a monstrous building, the 'slaughterhouse' women call it. There's a daily turn-over of two hundred to three hundred women there.

Each ward contains ten to fifteen curtained-off beds piled with flannelette blankets. There are never enough sheets and a woman has to make do with one, either covering herself with it or laying it under her. And this is in a medical institution where operations are carried out.

But the women in here don't notice such discomforts. They are consumed with terror as they await the forthcoming blasphemy. The crucial moment comes. The women line up outside the operating theatre.

Abortions are carried out on two, even on six women simultaneously in the same theatre. The tables are placed so that a woman can see everything that goes on opposite her: the face distorted in pain, the bloody mass extracted from the womb. In the theatre there are two doctors and one sister. "Hurry up now!" says the sister. The woman, trembling with fear and agitation, climbs onto the table, her movements clumsy and uncertain.

The doctor irritably tells her how she must lie on the table. Finally she is ready and the doctor begins to operate. Sometimes he gives her an injection but it has no effect because so little novocaine is used, and he doesn't wait for it to work anyway. As she isn't anaesthetised, the woman suffers terrible pain. Some lose consciousness. The sister is unable to help as she's assisting two doctors at the same time. The patient is 'pumped out' with difficulty, sent packing, and conducted past the women waiting their turn back to the ward. There she writhes with pain for perhaps another hour and a half, sick and occasionally vomiting. On the next day she is discharged without even a cursory glance at her general condition, and is left to hope for the best.

The health service in the Soviet Union merely dispenses charity, relying as it does on patients' ability to cure themselves. They're merely given first aid. For the rest they have to fend for themselves.

"Golden Childhood"

Vanya Pazukhin*

*Vanya is the diminutive of Ivan

My mother used to tell me how much fun it was at pioneer camps[1] when she was young, how there was lots to do, everyone was nice and friendly and she had a good time. I was really keen to go and everyone – my grandma, grandpa and my father – tried hard to fix me a place, but with no success. But as it happpened I kept getting ill and was off school all winter, and one fine day I found out that the clinic had decided to allocate me a place in a convalescent pioneer camp because of my poor health. When I went for my check-up, the doctors discovered that I had high leucocytes. I had surmounted one obstacle only to find myself confronted by a second: I thought this blood analysis might cost me my holiday. But when we went to see the woman in charge of the clinic she said it was of no importance whatsoever and it was quite alright to go.

And so one sunny day we arrived at the Zarnitsa camp in Staryi Petergof[2]. A very fat and ugly woman registered me and told me I would be in the pioneer group number eight. Lots of our women are fat so I did not pay any attention to the fact. We said goodbye to our parents and went off for lunch. As soon as our parents had gone, the teacher began to shout at us even though none of us had done anything wrong.

She spent all the dinner time telling us off, shouting and yelling, but I thought, all the same it was just this particular teacher and the children would be much nicer. After the meal it was our rest time. As I already said, my mother told me I would have a good time at the camp. Now, just as soon as the teacher had left the room, the boys began to tell each other dirty jokes. Then they jumped out of bed and began to thump each other. The fighting ended when two boys got hit really hard over the head and felt sick. Vladik had started the fight just for the fun of it. He was the son of the woman in charge of the camp and he used to say to us, "If you try hitting me and don't do as I say, I'll tell my mum and you'll get kicked out of the camp." After the fight the boys thought up a new game which they called 'the meat mincer'. The nine of them would stand in circles (there were ten of us in our room, but I didn't play games like that): a big circle, then a small circle and then one person in the very centre (Zhenya, the smallest boy in the room, who was nicknamed "the Georgian" always stood in the middle.) The idea was to clobber each other with their towels which they had first tied in knots and soaked in water. On this note the rest hour drew to a close.

Then it was time for our tea and after that we went out for a walk. Although there were beautiful woods and clumps of trees all around the camp, they only let us walk in the duty courtyard right in front of the building. Roads ran along all sides of the courtyard and ambulances were always racing up and down (they often came to the camp to take injured pioneers off to hospital). When we went out walking, the boys spent the whole time fighting or making 'explosives'. They would rest a board on top of a vertically-standing brick, wrap sand up in a burdock leaf, put it on one end of the board and jump on the other. The burdock leaf would fly high in the air, then start falling. As it opened up, the sand spurted out and upwards, then cascaded groundwards getting down people's backs and in their hair. The boys got most excited when they made a 'bonnet' ie when the burdock leaf fell on someone's head. Often it fell on the teacher's head, which was why they were so keen on the game in the first place.

After supper we went to bed. While the teacher was in the room, they all lay quietly like baby hares in their burrows. As soon as she had gone, the boys jumped up and started laying in to each other. Then they got fed up with this and got into bed for a couple of minutes. But suddenly Vladik had a bright idea: he had thought up a new game and began asking if anyone had any draughts. I kept quiet though I did have some. But they started searching in all the bedside cupboards and discovered my draughts. They took the box, tore it open, threw the draughts on the floor and started chucking them around. Then they opened the door wide and began to throw them out into the corridor. Then everyone got back into bed again. Suddenly the door burst open, the lock flew off and the boys from another group came in to summon us to battle. Boys were streaming out of the bedrooms with their towels soaking wet and tied in knots. They drew themselves up into lines in the corridor and started attacking each other, hitting each other over the head with the towels. There were eight or nine of these so-called armies. It was like the revolution, even the battlecries; the groups fell upon each other with shouts of 'Hurrah' and knocked down anything that got in their way.

You may well ask where the teachers were. They had gone home to Leningrad at nine o'clock. You may well say, and what about the caretaker? We did have one, but he was downstairs chasing the older boys who were pushing each other off the windowsills.

After the fight had died down, some of the boys heard footsteps and saw the caretaker coming. They started to scatter, calling out: "The panther" (that's what they called him) "the panther's coming". The boys rushed back into our room and got into bed. The caretaker came in. "Now, why aren't you lot asleep,"he said, "it's already two in the morning."

When he had gone, the boys went on talking a little, telling jokes. Gradually everyone dropped off to sleep.

In the morning we got up, had breakfast and went for a walk in our dusty courtyard. There was nothing at all for the pioneers to do, and so they were always getting up to nasty tricks. Once, I think it was the day before the parents' day, I was talking to a boy from another group and he told me the following story: a six-year old boy was just walking along the path. A big boy (a fifteen or sixteen year old) was walking behind him and another was walking towards him. The one behind pushed the little boy so that he fell forward and bumped into the one in front. This big boy took the little boy by the feet and with all his strength swung him against a wooden shelter that was standing close by. Blood gushed from the boy's head and he had to be taken to hospital. It is a pity that I don't know what happened to the boys who were responsible for this incident.

And one night Zhenya, the boy they called "the Georgian" was lying in bed sucking his comb. Another boy called Igor swiped Zhenya with a pillow so hard that the comb got stuck in his throat. Blood was gushing from Zhenya's mouth so he went to the doctor. But the doctor only yelled at him: "Why on earth do you come disturbing us in the middle of the night? We need our sleep as well you know."

In the morning they took Zhenya off to the hospital and I didn't see him again.

The only special classes organised at the camp were for making soft toys, but that was only for the girls. Later a drawing class was organised but out of the whole camp there were only four pioneers besides me who joined. No one else wanted to draw, no one was interested in the arts.

Outings were very rare. Twice we went to Peter's Palace and that was all. There was football, but that was only for boys who liked having fights. The football they played consisted of beating up the goal-keepers or kicking the ball so as to hit unsuspecting passers-by. That's not my kind of football.

One morning Vova came running into my room. Vova was the best person in the whole of the camp. He had the following story to tell me: a boy had been pushed against a wall so hard that he hit his nose, fell awkwardly and broke his arm. He was taken off to the hospital straight away, but nothing happened to the boy who had pushed him, he didn't even get a telling-off.

Then the boys from my room hid my sun hat. The teacher noticed that I was without it and made me wear a woollen cap even though it was hot. For three days, until our pioneer leader came back, I had to sit in the sun in this cap; it made me feel awful.

Once during the daytime rest our teacher called over her grandson from group three (the boys in this group were aged thirteen and fourteen), and he got his friends together. When they arrived, she said to us: "If you so much as move, they'll see you get a hiding".

These boys often used to come into our room during rest period and would do all sorts of naughty things. When we giggled they used to climb on top of us and start pummelling us – our faces and stomachs usually – with their fists.

In our group there was a girl called Sevda who used to get teased and called a darkie because she came from Central Asia. Sometimes she used to ask me for sweets and I would oblige. The other boys saw me and started to tease me as well and make fun of me every way they could. Once when it was my turn to do the cleaning and I was washing the floor, one of them grabbed my mop and threw it on the ground so that I had to bend down to pick it up. The idea was to humiliate me by making me kneel in front of him. And once when they were swinging to and fro on my bed – at night they were always jumping from bed to bed – they shifted my mattress. When I got up to put it right they did something to me that I don't even want to write about. And one of the boys pushed me so hard that I fell over and hit my back against the iron bedstead. My back started hurting and when I touched it I found blood on my hand.

After this had happened I didn't want to stay at the camp any longer, because I realised that the camp was only for very strong boys who liked fighting or swearing all the time. I asked my mother to take me home. This meant going to the director of the camp to ask permission. When I told the boys in my room that my mother was going to take me away on Sunday, Vladik, the son of the director of the camp said "I shall tell my mother not to let you leave".

When my mother decided to take me away, she went to see the director of the camp to ask permission. The director said that I was telling a pack of lies, that such dreadful things couldn't happen and that no one was getting hurt – although several boys had been taken away to hospital in front of her very eyes. So we had to slip away unnoticed – while no one was looking I packed my case and we made our escape.

And so I now call that place a concentration camp for pioneers. After my experience I have come to the conclusion that the next generation will terrorise the world; the earth will drip blood, and everything will be smothered in smoke and the only words spoken will be swear words. I used to think only the older generation was so bad and that the next generation would create a new life. But as it turns out I was quite wrong.

Notes

1 The pioneer movement is the official Soviet youth organisation and claims membership of over 99% of children between the ages of nine and fourteen. It is responsible for all organised social activities and also for political education. There are several thousand pioneer camps, providing holidays every year for over twenty million children. (The camps are mixed, though sleeping accommodation is separate.)

2 Staryi Petergof is a small town on the Gulf of Finland not far from Leningrad. The tsars had a palace there, Peter's Palace, which was destroyed by the Germans in the last war but is now rebuilt and open to the public.

Letter from Novosibirsk

J. Voznesenskaya

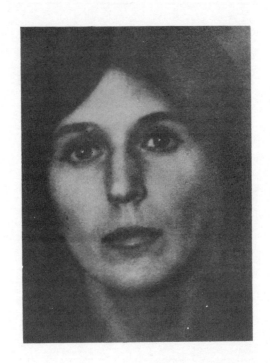

Well, now I've seen everything. The most awful things possible. There's nothing more for them to show me now. I could even go home. I have reached the edge and looked over. This is what happened . . . .

It was dead of night when they brought me and the woman I was travelling with to cell No.247. It was knee-deep in dirt. But we were worn out and climbed onto our *shkonki* (wooden plank beds) and fell fast asleep. The next morning we rolled up our sleeves and cleaned out these Augean stables of ours. We had only just begun a day in cleanliness when suddenly a party of prisoners arrived from the camp for young offenders in Tomsk.

They were an exceptionally picturesque crowd. They were all very beautiful young women. They had all just turned 18 and were being delivered to adult camps. You could tell they all got on very well with each other. One girl in the group had fallen ill so they practically carried her in their arms, laying her down on the best bunk, giving her tea, and wrapping her up in their own scanty clothing.

. . .

An hour later they were transferred to another cell.

On May 22 the woman travelling with me and I were told about our departure the next day and were taken to the baths. On the way we were joined by the same group of women who had been under-age offenders. The girl who was ill was still with them. She had a high temperature and was delirious, with sharp pains in her stomach and diahorrea. I asked them whether they had called a doctor. They said they had. The doctor had prescribed several tablets; she had said that the girl could continue with her journey.

We're a noisy pack as we sing and undress and are led to the shower. The shower room itself is about six metres long, eight at most. There are twenty of us. We're packed in solid. Suddenly the hot water starts gushing out. It's boiling hot. We rush to the side, screaming. A moment later, it's freezing water that's gushing out, then boiling again. It was actually boiling, Natasha, hot enough to scald you. At first, I thought there must be something wrong with the shower. With bare heels, I banged with all my strength against the door. A *mentovka* came (in this instance a woman - one of the guards). I explained that the shower had broken down, but she laughed. I shout at her in fury, "Open up at once!" Straightaway the water comes out at normal temperature. We recover our breath and start lathering our hair. But then suddenly everything stops - they've switched off the water altogether. "Come on out of there", someone shouts. But our hair is all soapy. We get hysterical, and demand that they turn the water on again. On it comes. Boiling hot. Then freezing. Again everyone is flat against the side, screaming, rubbing their eyes. The door is flung open, "Out you come!". Rinsing their faces in cold water as best they can, the girls run out into the corridor. My friend and I brave it out and wash off all the soap in cold water. The mentovka screams at us but we take no notice. The water dries up completely. It's only then that we leave. The girls are just outside in the corridor, crowding round the shower-room door, yelling as though wounded. We don't understand what's going on at all and stand in the door-way. Alongside a woman warder and a doctor — a man of around 25 — are standing. They both seemed rather pleased with themselves about something. The mentovka yells, "Move! Move! Nothing's going to happen to you!" The girls start running along the corridor. It turns out that there are male orderlies (convicts who act as cleaners, painters and decorators etc) lining the corridor. They stand and mock the poor things running past them. I realised a long time ago that washing always means being leered at, and I'd taken to the harmful precaution of always washing in a shirt. I didn't run, instead calmly walked out towards the men who were having such a good time and gave them a few tender words of my own. I then went up to the doctor and the warder and thanked them. "I've read of such things in Solzhenitsyn", I said, "I've seen similar scenes in Romm's *Everyday Fascism* but I never thought that I'd have the pleasure of being present at such fascist entertainment myself. Thank you very much for giving me such excellent material." They were quite taken aback and fell silent. Wagging my wet shirt tail I walked calmly down the corridor of men. Not one dog grins. And I was ready to snarl with hate. They'd made me shake all over, but not from the cold water.

We returned to our cell, packed our things ready for our departure the next day, and went to sleep. Suddenly during the night we hear cries coming from the young women's cell. Someone crying for her mother, but we could't catch anything else. Then everything was quiet again. But we couldn't sleep. A little later there were more cries. We decided that the women had probably been escorted off in their group, and we started to wait for them to come for us too. They were such noisy girls anyway that we didn't really think all that much about their shouting.

But the next day they were brought into our cell again and we straightaway found out what it had all been about. I've written it down for you from their own words.

On May 21 a party of 22 girls arrived at the Novosibirsk Prison from VTK-2 (a correction centre work camp). They were en route to adult work camps. Two of the girls had fallen ill. Liza Maksimova had had a heart attack,and Ira Krupyenkova was suffering from a fever and diahorrea (I've already mentioned her. There is now an epidemic of gastric infection in the area. Everywhere is in quarantine.) There was no help offered from the doctors in Novosibirsk. The girls weren't taken out of the party. In the morning they took the young women to the baths. Later that day they were told that they would be setting off for another camp the next morning. According to the rules, everyone has to have a shower before leaving. So that evening they were taken to the baths for a second time. They didn't want to go and explained that they had already washed that morning. Nevertheless they were all forced to go. Even the sick Ira Krupyenkova. I've already told you about the free striptease show — I too was a victim of that humiliation, aimed at the defenceless younger women.

After their bath some of the girls went straight to bed, and others began preparing for their departure. That day they had been singing and there had been a scene about it with a warder. The young women told me that no-one had stopped them singing in the camp they had come from and they had not paid any attention to what the warder had said. They couldn't believe that you weren't allowed to sing in prison. The chief warder threatened them with reprisals. "You don't yet know how things work here," he said, "But I'll give you a little demonstration as a farewell."

That evening none of the girls were singing. There wasn't even much chatter. They were getting ready for their departure.

Twelve o'clock that night the door opened and two of the warders came in with a fire hose in their hands. "We'll organise a farewell dip for your departure", they announced. More warders were in the corridor.

The two came into the cell and began drenching the girls, chasing them around the cell with the force of the water. Many of the girls were half undressed. Then one of the men doused the girls and beat them about whilst the other threw them out one by one out into the corridor. There the prison reserves, summoned by the warder on duty, were standing in two ranks. The girls had to run down between the two lines of about 24 men. They were hit with fists, hoses, keys. Then they were chased down basement corridors towards the solitary confinement cells. These corridors were damp and dirty with pools of water on the floor and almost no light. The girls were running half-naked, bare-foot; the ones that were ill running along with the others. Coming out of the basement they were chased into the corridor with the solitary confinement cells. The beasts overtook them by another corridor and waited for them, forming into two ranks again. Once more the girls had to pass down between the rows. They were then locked into in a solitary confinement cell designed for four people — 21 girls in all (one had been shut in a cell by herself the day before for fighting in the cell — I think so at least). The men remarked to one another that they had better get some of the girls to clean out their cell. So they let out five of them and took them back to the cell saying, "If you've not cleaned it out within ten minutes there'll be a repeat." In the cell the table was upturned, the beds flooded and the water on the floor was ankle-deep. The girls were frightened of talking in the solitary confinement cell, even in a whisper. They began to suffocate (even on your own in these cells there's only enough air to breathe for half an hour). They could hear mocking taunts and threats coming from the corridor. They were threatened with handcuffs, straitjackets, more beatings. Ten minutes later everyone was suffocating. The first to lose conssciousness was Sveta Medvedyeva. The women began banging on the door, begging to be released and for Sveta to be let out. "Wait till she's snuffed it — then we'll open up", came the reply. But 15 minutes later the door was opened and the woman warder on duty had Sveta put on the floor and the others were ordered back into the cell.

Sveta came round in the medical centre. Doctors looked at her record and found that she was ill. They inquired why she was travelling without a doctor. While Sveta was there the medical centre were informed by telephone that Natasha Kachulina was having an epileptic fit (she has suffered from epilepsy since childhood). The doctor told the warder over the telephone, "They're getting their just deserts. Anyway, they make it up."

(I was asked an interesting question the following day when I demanded that the doctor in charge of the medical centre examine all the women who had been beaten up and begin an investigation. She asked, "Aren't you curious as to why it happened? Maybe they deserved it!" And it was only once they were sure that in this instance the girls had not committed any particular offence, that they began an investigation, interrogating all the girls who'd been injured and promising to punish the guilty parties. Oh, I don't believe in their promises — and the authorities were not at all surprised by the incident.)

A second woman who was also an epileptic began an attack and they refused to give her any medical help. The illnesses of both women were recorded on file — but they keep their own files!

Tanya Tapenya had an asthma attack. She fell to the floor, and began thrashing about, tearing at her mouth with her fingers, and then lost consciousness. Again the girls began banging on the walls of the cell. The door opened and all three were allowed to be carried out. They were thrown out onto the cold, cement floor. In the cold they regained consciousness and were immediately ordered into another cell. They had no strength left. They were shouted at and threatened. They crawled along the floor on all-fours towards the appointed cell. A male warder and two mentovkas were in the corridor. They made insulting remarks and laughed at the girls crawling on all fours, unable to walk on their feet. They were called dogs, bitches and all manner of foul names. Tanya Tapenya kept saying the same thing over and over again to herself — "Never, never have I been so humiliated."

The three were locked in a large cell. But it had a wet cement floor, covered in water. And in their present state they couldn't get up from the floor.

Back in the small cell the next to lose consciousness was Ira Rusack, an absolutely healthy young woman. Then Ira Yeveseva. The girls banged on the walls for about 25 minutes. Then the door opened and they were told to get out. They were put in the cell with the other three. They remained there till morning, standing and sitting on the wet cement floor. There were two benches, but they couldn't all sit on them. Sveta was brought in from the medical centre. Zhenya Vlasova got cramps in her legs. At five the next morning they couldn't hold out any longer and began banging on the walls again (some had just bras and pants on. One had only a pair of pants on, and they were all obviously wet through.) The warder appeared, and told them that if they banged on the wall again they'd have to stay there all day too. They were finally let out at breakfast time. Back in the cell they fell asleep on their wet mattresses.

When the girls were brought into our cell that evening, a lot of their clothes were still damp — their trousers and jumpers (not all of them had a change of clothes). I of course made a fuss and assured them that corporal punishment is forbidden in adult prisons. They were real children. Many of them have been in the detention centre for three or four years and have absolutely no preparation for adult life. "At the detention centre we lived like at pioneer camp. We had to be clean and well-disciplined, but we were treated like children. No-one humiliated us." They smoke. They even swear. But they are even more childlike than children who've never been in prison. They tremble with fear, helpless, not knowing where to find protection. What is worse, this incident at Novosibirsk Prison was not the first of its kind. These same girls were beaten up when they were still minors, some of them.

Tanya Tapenya tells her story. In December 1975 a party was taken to Tomsk, to the VTK. In cell No.245 the same incident was repeated with fire hoses and assault. The women who had 'sinned' by asking for a doctor to examine their sick friend who was suffering from a congenital heart complaint (Tanya Tapenya doesn't remember her name). The doctor told them they were playing him up. They then had water poured all over them and they were chased down the corridor. They handcuffed Pushkareva, the Shatsky girls, and Pavlenko. Galya Pavlenko, Katya Khalilova, Vera Titova, Lida Shoffyor and Lyuba Myakshina were there. All these women were later in VTK-2 in Tomsk.

In November 1976 again a similar incident. One night all the lights in the prison went out. The girls kicked up a racket, screaming with fear — for they did not know that the lights had gone out everywhere, and they were frightened that the lights in their cell had been deliberately switched off. Again, the prison reserves were summoned and the girls had to pass through their ranks. Then, as on the other occasion, they were kept in a cell till morning. Ira Rusack, Ira Olyechik and Anya Artemyeva were all there.

I'm now setting off with these girls to Irkutsk. Many of them have bad coughs and sore throats. Natasha Kachulina is flat on her back, very pale and cannot get up or eat. Tamara Tapelova (she was barefoot and had only her pants on the night of the incident) is now suffering from much worse rheumatism. Ira Krupyenkova is in a very grave condition (it's four days since she last ate and that was on the night of the incident). Everyone has chest infections and hoarse voices. They're all feeling deeply humiliated.

Natasha! Everyone must get to hear of this incident, or we will be worth nothing.

The poster woman/short story

I. Tishchenko

Her drawings are the embodiment of dynamics. Movement is the expression of her face. Her long fingers are restless. She is the most motor-mad person I know. Paralysed when she was nineteen years old. She was too fond of her motor, her steed – a moped, bought with her first earnings. She pasted up posters. Those solitary and clear mornings when you are alone with your fantasies. The bright posters are like patches of rainbow in the mist. The little town lies in a valley. There are often mists in the valley. So there she was with her moped and some players from the visiting "Chapiteau" circus. The players were on paper, the moped real. She loved it too much and once it abused her trust. Irredeemably. For ever. Or was the cause of it the mist? Only at that moment suddenly for the first time everything stood still. Everything that lived. Everything that was part of that incessant movement which delighted her, which was essential to her... Everything stopped. Her heart stopped. Clinical death. That is past. Past is the operation on her spine. All the fragments of bone were carefully pulled out of the spinal cord, but the spine refused to function. It had set. Frozen. Stiffened. Her life in a chair began. All the movement contained in her being was concentrated in her eyes. Even when they, those eyes, looked steadily into yours, they seemed potentially to be preparing for movement. All the emotions which could be expressed and which it would seem are impossible to express – they expressed. The movement emanating from her pupils was, as before, infectious. It infected us, who could walk.

And she drew posters:
Flying – the pigeons from under the magician's hands
Flying – the hands of the dance-pianist
Flying – the eyelids of the spectators
following with bated breath the flight of the trapeze artists Flying away
the plane that was taking her to yet another town, where they again
refused a repeat operation – too dangerous!
But she would not give up.

73

Flying on her poster, a new sun.

And in her chair, like the captain of a ship, she directed the world of her fantasies. Before she had not drawn, but movement was her essence, her foundation – it had to burst out in something.

And so was born the dynamic of lines, the play of colour. And somewhere, pulled out of her skull, tight-rope walkers continued to balance, wheels spun, performing dogs jumped, clowns tumbled on sawdust, fighting cocks flashed, jugglers handled their props, tigers bared their teeth, trick riders galloped by, motorcycles soared up in the ring of death, ridden by the celebrated mother and daughter . . .

Now I have become the poster woman in our little town. I visit the home of this remarkable person, who conceals an explosion within herself, and I periodically despise myself for leading a life that's too quiet and measured. Maybe I should buy a moped?

Flying lizards/ short story

S. Sokolova

The little man hung by one drawing pin and smiled.

His smile went diagonally from top to bottom.

It seemed that the little man was happy precisely because he was hanging in such an unusual manner. The sheet of paper onto which the little man was stuck was called a collage. To start with it had been level, firmly fixed to the wall by two drawing pins.

In time one pin fell and was lost, so the little man had to hang crookedly.

The collage was made by Serezha.

He cut out of paper a red triangle and a yellow square, stuck them onto thick white paper – and it was a house.

Soon a black chimney appeared by the house. Puffs of black, pencilled smoke started to come from it.

Then a little man appeared and, finally, some stars. The stars were big and round, like balloons, and in just as many colours – red, yellow, blue. They tumbled from top to bottom and hit the roof of the house.

When they hit it, a sound could clearly be heard: bing-bang-bong.

But for some reason no one except Serezha heard the stars falling.

But he heard it loud and clear: bing-bang-bong.

The sun was also hanging there.

It had two eyes and a red, smiling mouth – the sun was laughing.

Above it were stripes – the blue sky.

The little man pushed his head against the stars.

He was wearing a kaftan with yellow buttons.

He had one hand stretched towards the house, as if he was inviting guests: "Come in, whoever wishes, come to my house". But there was no way he could have got in himself – the house was much too small.

Africa was also hanging there – blue palm trees on red paper. Among the blue palm trees lions and tigers roamed. Just like the ones in the zoo. Only real ones.

True, no one ever saw them, not even Serezha. But that was because in the day-time they hid in the bushes and came out to hunt at night, when everyone was asleep.

Serezha visited Africa together with Mama.

When Mama collected Serezha from the nursery she always asked: "Well, Serezha, where shall we go today?"

And Serezha invariably replied: "Let's go to Africa, like we always do".

Africa was on the other side of the house.

It was a huge country overgrown with nettles, burdock and thorns.

Fallen leaves rustled under their feet – hidden beneath them were snakes and boa constrictors.

Once he even caught sight of a king python – it was hanging from a tree.

True, when Serezha went a little nearer the python suddenly turned itself into a branch. But that was from fear, in case Serezha picked it up and carried it away.

Because when Serezha went away it calmed down and became a python once again.

But most importantly of all – in Africa there were flying lizards.

These ancient lizards had long ago died out everywhere. Only Serezha had them, in Africa.

Serezha knew from Mama that they had died out.

Mama worked in an institute where they stuffed different animals. Once she brought Serezha a big book with bright pictures. In one picture there was a drawing of a big bird, like a flying mouse, only it had a long nose like a stork's and big, sharp teeth.

Serezha looked at the picture in amazement: "What an interesting bird! I've never seen one like that, not even in the zoo."

"Those are ancient flying lizards", explained Mama, "They died out long, long ago."

"But such big interesting birds can't be all dead?" Serezha almost burst into tears. "Maybe there's just one left? I'd only want to see it just once."

Serezha looked pleadingly at Mama. Mama smiled: "Well, let's pretend they've died out everywhere, but in our Africa they're still alive. And we're going to hunt them."

But hunting them was not quite so simple.

Because they weren't really lizards, but sparrows. And as soon as Serezha ran out from behind the bushes, they all flew away.

On the whole, it was fun playing with Mama.

Mama was dark, with long black plaits. For some reason her hair always smelt of flowers.

Serezha once asked: "Mama, why does your hair always smell so beautiful, like flowers?"

Mama laughed: "Not beautiful, but nice. And it doesn't smell of flowers, it's shampoo."

Mama was so brown that everyone thought she had just come from the south.

And had done nothing there but sunbathe.

When they were coming out of the cinema some man or other even came right up to her and asked: "Where did you get so brown? I suppose you've just come from the south?"

Mama smiled: "Me? I'm from Africa."

The man looked at her rather strangely and then asked cautiously: "What were you doing there?" Mama calmly replied: "Hunting lions."

The man didn't ask anything else and for some reason quickly walked off. Mama laughed for a long time.

They also took the cat, Vas'ka, hunting with them.

He hunted like a real cat – when the flying lizards came down to a clearing, he pressed himself to the ground and his eyes lit up.

But he wasn't really a cat.

He was a prince, turned into a cat by a wicked wizard.

But he didn't know this himself.

In fact, no one knew except Serezha. It was his secret. Mama was the only person he once told.

Mama thought for a moment: "Yes, poor Vas'ka.

But you know, I once read in some old books that there's a special herb that can undo any spell.

When we go to the countryside on Sunday, we'll look for it."

But they never went to the countryside on Sunday.

On Sunday Papa returned from his *kommandirovka* (work or study trip).

Papa went into the room and immediately said: "What's this nonsense? What have you gone and hung on the wall? It's tasteless."

Why does it have to have taste? Do you eat collage? It's simply there for decoration.

Papa tore it all down and threw it in the rubbish bin.

Africa disappeared, the little man disappeared, the stars stopped falling down.

Serezha became very, very sad. Suddenly he wanted to cry. "Don't get upset, son", Papa comforted him. "I'll buy you a clockwork tank instead."

There will be no more pythons, lions, and flying lizards.

Goodbye, Africa!

ПОЭЗИЯ

ТАТЬЯНА МАМОНОВА

Poetry

Tatyana Mamonova

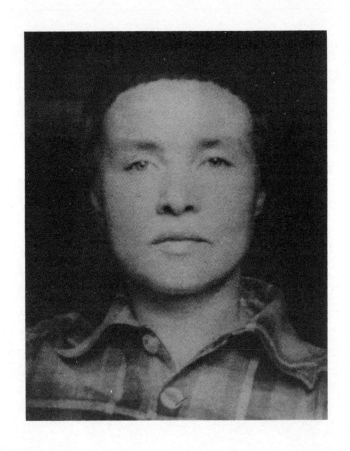

Everyday life is torture
the old chargers' hooves are worn down
I long to leave the house –
And you really have never known
whose whiteness drives me out?
The brilliance of paper
is the purest of murky water!

A dying cry
in the high ceilings above
steps running through unlit rooms –
Who was running there yesterday?
Who was hungry there yesterday?
Now it is empty in the rooms above
and only the cracks in the ceiling
recall to mind that frozen cry –
Who was running there yesterday?
Who was hungry there yesterday?

The question remains
on the icon's face.

Fugitive woman
scorning hell
bright in the light of day,
when you entered into this garden
you looked at me so wisely.
Yet etched in the depths of your eyes
there was night,
discovered traces of hell.

But floating high above your head
was a colonnade of clouds.
This floating vault will not collapse
you are not in its power,
for you have tasted the shattering power
of the waters there!

Petals from the appletrees' branches
flutter like snow to our feet,
and the noisy warbling of birdsong
wafts to us from heaven . . .
To speak aloud of this quiet joy
is not a waste of speech.
Why waste your barefoot song
on those who are deaf?
This friend will not be afraid
of your fears and griefs,
for in her hands she holds
the girths of your true fate.
Her horses will not bolt
restrained by her command,
while with ceremonious solemnity
and an essence of ice
she winds up the clock –
and the horses of fortune are released.

The actor is triumphant
but the housewife weeps!

We have too much in common
for me not to be afraid of you.
We were once fortune-tellers
but were banished by the scent of acacia.
Thenceforth we became doubles –
your duality flows within me,
we have only our diaries in which to conceal
the yellowing pages of our souls.

Gallop away the miles
past a trickle of river.
The sky falls into the horses' manes,
our hands are full of snow.
The guests, sated with the chase,
are drunker than honey.

Dreams and divinations
I do not ask of you.
The loaves were eaten in the morning,
tomorrow the Saviour comes.
The old unreasoning evil
was merely reduced to the oprichnina[1] –
we have simply been lucky.
Secrets, your old clothes,
I do not ask of you.
The wind lashes the branches
and beats on my window all morning.

I fear decrepitude.
I follow that old woman –
for I may be warned a little –
walking as if to fetch water.
Behind me darkness is falling,
before me straight ahead
lies the road to hell . . .

But you were born for this life
and must endure for now all its troubles.
Do not ask for forgiveness
for the candle has been extinguished
and the food on the table is cold.
Alone now – for all are asleep –
she greedily gulps in the silence.
The tram is singing its last couplet:
look after your faithful wife,
and hide yourself from yourself
under your old grey rug.
Oh this night is blessed
for the agitated soul
who cannot find a home –
write,
write your poems, write,
and do not be too stern a judge
on one so close to you.

A bird falls from a bush
into the darkness of space –
I have no strength to resist
these empty depths of night!
I fall flying into you –
I am a sundered tree
showering splinters like birds as I crash
shattering the space on my left,
while again on my right the lightning strikes
and once again shatters me.

I shall know the measure of this earth
when I have forgotten pain.

The winged leaves of the maples
like driven flocks of birds
scorched yellow by Septembers
spin headlong to the ground.

Mahadevi

E. Shvartz

Not from one, not from three
But from eighty-three hundred thousand mothers
I have pushed my way onto this earth.
And I have lived different lives
In many dissimilar worlds.
Now I have sated my hunger
For happiness and grief.
Whatever my lives may have been
Take pity on me today,
Oh God white as jasmine!

Maya[3] clings to me
Like the shadow of my body,
The heart of my life,
The memory of my heart –
And now conscience come to my memory.
She grazes the worlds with raised staff,
Who will conquer her, God white as jasmine,
If it was You who created her?

Rather than always live together
Let us for a short while part.
The joy of our meeting is greater
After these times spent apart.

But to part from Him
Is not to be born,
We cannot escape from His gaze.

Friend! How can we deceive one another –
Or part
Or pine
Or be happy
At the premonition of a parting
With God white as jasmine?

Can the warm sheltering sky
Know the secrets of the cosmos?
Only the moon knows.

Can the willow by the river
Know how deep is the water?
Only the lotus knows.

And the fly, can it know
The flower's secret sweetness?
Only the bee knows.

Oh God, white as jasmine,
Only thou canst know
The path of the truly devout.

How can these creatures know –
These gnats on an ox's flank?

Listen sister, listen,
I have had a dream:

I dreamt of rice
And betel-nut,
A palm-leaf
And a coconut.
And I saw an ascete
Begging for his food.
His teeth were white,
His clothes were in rags,
His curling hair was uncombed.
And following in his heels
I took him by the hand,
This destroyer of worlds.
God white as jasmine
I have seen
In a dream
Not in a dream, in a dream.

His curling hair was russet
A diadem was on his head
His small teeth gleamed as he laughed
His eyes were flooded with light,
The light of fourteen worlds.
My eyes have feasted their fill,
I have seen God in His glory.

I have seen a proud God –
For Him only men are people
And woman for him is dumb.

I saw the primordial being
In the ardent embraces of Shakhti.[4]

This gapana[5] is part of Alama's[6] reply to Mahadevi:
Alama asks her why, if she stands above all conventions, she still covers
her body with her long braids. Mahadevi replies that the fruit can be
peeled only when it is ripe, and Alama says: "You do not know whether
God is within you or you are in God. If the fruit is peeled too early, the
juice is bitter".

> If
> You tear out the fang of a snake
> And charm it with your pipe
> The snake becomes more beautiful.
> If you revere your body
> Your body will be beautiful.
> The untrue body is like a mother
> Transformed into a vampire.
>
> Oh God, white as jasmine,
> For those that love Thee there is no body!

> To appease my hunger
> I have a few handfuls of rice –
> The alms they gave me in town.
>
> To appease my thirst
> I have streams and wells and ponds.
>
> And to soothe me to sleep
> I have the ruins of temples.
>
> And I have a friend,
> I have you
> God white as jasmine!

I do not need
This foolish dying world
This pot of night illusions
This haunt of hideous passions.
I do not need
This broken cracked old pot
Leaking out the day,
I do not need it.
Did I choose it?

Take it quickly away then,
Blow a hurricane, snatch it up,
And blow it away,
Oh God white as jasmine!

According to legend, this was written on the Shrisail mountain shortly before her death:

Brothers, do not squander your strength
Of what do you need to convince
This wrinkled old woman
So dishevelled and faded?

Why trouble yourselves for her, fathers?
She has no will
No strength left in her body,
The world she has forgotten
And she has lost herself.

Deprived of caste
She has made her nest
With God white as jasmine.

Where were You
When I knew not myself?

You dwelt in me
Like gold in gold.

How did You work this miracle
Concealing Yourself in me,
Invisible to the world,
Oh God white as jasmine?

Let a rainstorm hollow the sky
And wash clean my body,

Let a stone roll down the hill
And make a flower for my hair,

And Oh God white as jasmine,
If my head falls from my shoulders,
This is my sacrifice to You.

Notes
1 Oprichnina – Ivan the Terrible's personal secret police.
2 Mahadevi – the 'Great Goddess' of Hindu religion; representative of divine energy, and mate and counterpart to Siva the Great God.
3 Maya – illusion, ie the universe of phenomena, perceived as illusory when compared to the absolute totality of Brahman.
4 "Siva and Shakhti represent God and the Creative Force, the primordial pair (in tantra and yoga)" Elena Schwartz.
5 Gapana – an anecdote, or piece of gossip.
6 Alama – possibly a personification of Brahman.

"With the grandeur of Homer and the purity of Sappho . . ."

Ivina Tallin

For the title of my essay I've taken John Updike's words, with which he described Vladimir Nabokov's novel *Ada*. I'm not going to attempt to write about *Ada* – Updike has already done that. I merely want to draw the reader's attention to the distinctiveness and undoubted precision of the attribute 'sapphic purity'. It is sufficient unto itself, whatever might be added on to it – it is an indestructible phrase. Set side by side, these two words not only do not contradict each other, but rather one reinforces the other. Having dared to touch on this theme, I have intentionally chosen two poets who are stylistically very different. But surely a difference in style or period doesn't hinder a spiritual affinity. I have chosen true poets, for whom it is unimportant to which nation they belong, or to which sex, or which century. And so, we have Marina Tsvetaeva – a woman, a Russian woman of the twentieth century, and Walt Whitman, a man, a nineteenth century American. Both are brilliant articulators of a cosmic consciousness, of the intuitive thought of Poetic foresight. Without violence these poets tear up (blow up!) the accustomed boundaries of earthly existence. And if they are unable to liberate other people from invisible chains – that is not their fault. In order to free oneself, the other person must also become a Poet. Then, intoxicated with life, he pulsates on meeting it:

> "Passing stranger! you do not know
> how ardently, how longingly I look
> upon you.
> You must be he I was seeking everywhere
> somewhere
> I ate with you and slept with you
> Your body has become not yours only
> nor left my body mine only . . . "

That's Walt Whitman. This is Marina Tsvetaeva:

> "You pass along on your way

And I don't even touch your hand,
but there is an anguish inside of me –
it is so endless,
would that you were to me like anyone else.

Straight away my heart cried out 'beloved',
For you it was just something passing
but I've said farewell now,
Knowing nothing, not even your name!
O, love me, just love me!..."

The soul has no gender; this is the fundamental starting point of a true Poet. In the West, currently, they use the enigmatic symbol 'bi' (bisexual). Shame is hidden behind the brevity and reserve of this symbol. But this concept (of bisexuality) was absolutely indisputable for the American bard.

"To walk for a time amongst the people,
To touch their bodies
To embrace now male, now female flesh
with my hands,
what more could I want..."

In quite a different voice, but about that theme, Marina speaks:

"There are names like sultry blossoms,
And looks there are, like a flame...
There are dark, sinuous mouths
With deep, moist corners.

There are women with hair like helmets,
Whose fans waft fatally, delicately,
Perhaps they are thirty years of age,
Why are you one of them?
Why is mine the soul of a Spartan child?"

Let me repeat that my task isn't a comparison of Marina Tsvetaeva and Walt Whitman. But let there be for you, as there was for me, the joyful discovery of the unified nature of poetry, of the world of a poet. The poet allows the outside world to enter him, as it is, she opens herself out to the universe. There are no barriers for the poet, no restrictions.

"Women! why are you ashamed:
You are the gateway of the body
Even more, you are the gateway to the soul
A woman is like the seed,
The child is born unto a woman
The man is born unto the woman."

For a poet the body is sacred: "If my body is not the soul, what then is my soul?" One can determine a poet by her unerring precision:
"I love you! – it's like a
            thundercloud
Like a sin above you!
Because you're biting and burning hot
And better than all the rest.

I love you because you and I are
            different,
Our lives diverge in the darkness
            of the byways,
And for your inspired temptations
            and your dark fate . . .

I love you for this trembling,
Because surely I must be dreaming?
And for this lovely irony
That you're you – and not him."

Poets solve the riddle of 'sexual enigma'. Through love they have freed themselves from all kinds of fetters. Native moments are a catharsis for them – a cleansing, a fiery illumination of life's turmoil. Whether the poet turns to a 'crucified woman' or to a friend, his integrity is unblemished:
"This is a female body,
And I am like a helpless mist
            over it
And then everything falls away from me,
Everything disappears."

"You are silent,
You for whom I wandered
everywhere, often,
Only so that I could be near you . . .
but it didn't occur to you then,
What a subtle, electric fire
            burned in me,
Because of you."

Poets foretell the future. Not for a minute do they forget that round about us are myriad worlds, behind us myriad centuries. They understand that the mankind of the future will need a tradition of democratic friendship, for more and more, in the hearts of people, there grows a new delicacy, a love of one's comrade, one's companion, of like-minded people. Whoever follows in the footsteps of the poet is torn from the lacklustre mass of ordinary men.

"I remember with what sort of face
       you entered,
Without even the slightest blush,
How you rose, biting your finger,
Barely inclining your head.

Your brow, with love for power
       stamped on it
Lies there
Beneath the weight of a reddish
       mask,
Neither a woman nor a boy
But something stronger than me.

I rose with an unaccustomed movement,
They had surrounded us,
And in a joking tone someone said:
'Let me introduce you, ladies and gentlemen!'

And with a drawn-out movement you placed
       your hand in mine
On my palm there tenderly lingered
   A splinter of ice.

Already anticipating a clash,
With a sort of sideways glance
I half reclined in the chair,
Twisting the ring on my finger.

You took out a papirosi,
And I extended a match to you
Not knowing what I should do
Were you to look me
Straight in the face . . . "

The charm of a different soul, a fascination with the very being, the
essence of the spirit – this is the source of the poet's penchant for exalted
friendships. This passionate attraction of the Poet for another person,
regardless of that person's sex, frightened Whitman's first commentators,
accustomed as they were to the hypocritical reticence of their century and
to its limitations. Not without alarm did they quote some of his more
ardent lines from the cycle *Calamus*:
   "Whoever you are holding me now in hand,
   Without one thing all will be useless,
   I give you fair warning before you attempt me further,
   I am not what you supposed, but far different.

Who is he that would become my follower?

The way is suspicious, the result uncertain, perhaps
        destructive,
You would have to give up all else, I alone would expect
        to be your sole and exclusive standard,
Your novitiate even then would be long and exhausting,
Therefore release me now before troubling yourself any
        further, let go your hand from my shoulders,
Put me down and depart on your way.

Or else by stealth in some wood for trial,
Or back of a rock in the open air,
But just possibly with you on a high hill, first watching
        lest any person for miles around approach unawares,
Or possibly with you sailing at sea, or on the beach of
        the sea or some quiet island,
Here to put your lips upon mine I permit you,
With the comrade's long-dwelling kiss or the new husband's
        kiss,
For I am the new husband and I am the comrade.
Or if you will, thrusting me beneath your clothing,
Where I may feel the throbs of your heart or rest upon
        your hip . . . "

Nowadays, when in the States and Europe they talk so much about
'gay liberation', Marina Tsvetaeva's cycle of verses *The Woman Friend*
aren't treated so severely:
        "I see your lips are sinuous
        They reinforce your haughtiness,
        And the way your rather severe brow protrudes
        Grips my heart – takes it by storm!

        Your dress is like a black silk coat of mail,
        Your voice has the slightest touch of huskiness,
                like a gypsy's,
        Everything about you drives me to distraction,
        Even the fact that you're not beautiful! . . .

        You act the fool, be it with your fan, or with
                your walking stick,
        In every fibre and every little bone,
        In the shape of every naughty finger,
        There's the delicacy of a woman, the impertinence
                of a boy.
        I parry all your smiles with verse,
        I open out the whole world to you

Everything is in store for us from you,
Unknown woman, with the brow of Beethoven!"

This is not infamous 'sex', it is the dynamics of sex, it is the equivalent movement of the soul. It is interesting that in their private lives both Whitman and Tsvetaeva were intentionally, exaggeratedly upright. The poet is simply calling things by their proper names, not veiling or defiling those things. And any object to which the Poet turns, blazes with triumphant brilliance:

"Close, so closely above you
Do I whisper with my lips.
I have loved many men and women,
But none as I've loved you."

I beg you to excuse the number of quotes, but I wanted not so much to speak for the poets, as to let them speak for themselves, the more so since our reading public barely has access to them.

"Even on the eve of separation,
At love's ending,
I say again that I have loved these hands,
Your masterful hands.

And your eyes have I loved,
Demanding an account of any stray glance,
Not favouring someone – or anyone
With a look.

I love every bit of you,
You with that accursed passion –
God sees it! –
Demanding retribution
For any chance sigh . . . "

Our Appeal

Dear Sisters!

Hardly have we started out on life before we experience the full weight of women's destiny. At first we believe that the circumstances that hem us in, hurt us and humiliate us are accidental. It is inconceivable that they should be otherwise; that life should punish innocent people just because they happen to be born female. Humankind considers suffering inaccept- able and takes immediate steps to eliminate it wherever it appears. All suffering, that is, except the suffering of women. Our miseries are so unbearable that they must, one might suppose, disappear of their own accord, vanish like a bad dream. Nothing however changes by itself and we are convinced that no one will help us unless we help ourselves. Only by meeting together to discuss our bitterness and pain, only by exchanging our experiences and understanding them, can we find solutions to our problems. Only then shall we be able to help ourselves and the thousands of women who like us are unhappy. That is why we have decided to bring out our country's first free journal for women. Its pages will examine the position of women in the family, at work, in hospitals and maternity homes, the lives our children lead, and the question of women's moral rights. We shall publish articles and fiction written by women and also the personal histories of modern women.

We ask you to write to us about the things that worry you, the things you feel most strongly about. Send us articles you have written, stories about your sisters, mothers and women friends. If needs be, the women from our journal will come and see you and give whatever help they can. We hope that by pooling our efforts we can rekindle support for the forgotten cause of women's liberation and give women a new courage. After all: "Where there is light, there is hope".